FOR THE SAKE OF THE
CHURCH

POWER HOUSE

FOR THE SAKE OF THE
CHURCH

DR. MARY ANN SHEALY LANGSTON

Dedication

This book is dedicated to my husband, Deacon James H. (Jimmy) Langston, Jr.

I am so blessed to have your love, assistance, respect, and support. You have always encouraged me to fulfill my dreams and goals, and I am forever grateful. I am also thankful for our fifty-seven years of marriage (as of this writing) filled with love and support.

You are my *Gentle Giant*. Whatever I accomplish, I will share the journey and reward with you.

Always and forever,
I love you, Jimmy.

Contents

Acknowledgments

I give honor and praises to my Lord and Savior, Jesus Christ, for allowing me to complete this milestone. He has provided me with everything and everyone that I needed during this time. While I cannot acknowledge every individual who has impacted my life, I do thank each of you for your prayers and words of encouragement.

To my children, Jacintia, James III (Ultra), and Jameka, I love you; thanks for your sacrifices, unconditional love, and support. To my grandchildren, Jacquita, Jayla, Jayson, Jahquan, and Jayana; my great-grandchildren, Jeremiah, Justin, and Jayda; to Maxine and Junius (Beulah) Shealy, my Langston family in-laws, The House of Prayer Body of Christ (Dudley, North Carolina), and other supportive family and friends, thanks! I love you.

I offer my most profound appreciation and honor to my pastor, Apostle Dr. Michael E. Artis, and Lady Davilyn Artis for their encouragement, love, support, and especially their apostolic walk with our Savior. Also, I thank Dr. Gloria Anderson (pastor of New Apostolic Shiloh Holiness Church, Jacksonville, Florida) for her prophetic words of encouragement from before I began this project until its completion. You never gave up on me!

Finally, I honor and acknowledge in loving memory of my Granny (Bertha Braswell Jones Green), my parents, Junius Nathaniel Shealy Sr. and Bertha Mae Jones Shealy, and my parents-in-law, James Hamilton Langston, Sr., and Luberta Co-ley Langston. I honor the impact in my life of Pastor Moses H. Darden (founder of The House of Prayer, Dudley, North Carolina) and Lady Annie Ruth Darden, who adopted us as their spiritual children and were instrumental in our lives until their deaths. I acknowledge in remembrance Larry Williams, Jr., Deacon Marion (Pete) Barnes, and Jarvis L. Bizzell, my be-loved son-in-law.

I am forever grateful for you all. To God be the glory. He has given me great gifts, and He keeps doing great things in my life!

Introduction

Jesus Christ introduced us to the importance and future of the church in Matthew 16:18 when he declared to Peter that "the gates of hell shall not prevail against it." This brief statement provided us with the insight that a battle would be involved (and so it has continued, the devil against Jesus and His Body, those who are saved). But the prevailing truth is that through victory in Jesus Christ, we *have been made* winners and overcomers!

Yes, we know that the church has faced many tests and trials since its beginning, yet it continues to prevail! We don't have to fear the devil. The same God that fought for the inhabitants of Judah and Jerusalem is on our side.

> And he said, Hearken ye, all Judah, and ye inhabitants of Jerusalem, and thou king Jehoshaphat, Thus saith the LORD unto you, Be not afraid nor dismayed by reason of this great multitude; for the battle is not yours, but God's.

> To morrow go ye down against them: behold, they come up by the cliff of Ziz, and ye shall find them at the end of the brook before the wilderness of Jeruel.

Ye shall not need to fight in this battle: set yourselves, stand ye still, and see the salvation of the LORD with you, O Judah and Jerusalem: fear not, nor be dismayed; to morrow go out against them: for the LORD will be with you. (2 Chronicles 20:15–17)

Isn't that comforting? We don't have to fight to win or even to thrive! Because of God! He always has a remnant of disciples who have not bowed to satan. As believers in Christ, we must prepare ourselves to stand in these last and perilous times.

We cannot engage in common or natural warfare; our fight must be in the spiritual realm and according to the word of God.

For though we walk in the flesh, we do not war after the flesh: (for the weapons of our warfare are not carnal, but mighty through God to the pulling down of strong holds;) casting down imaginations, and every high thing that exalteth itself against the knowledge of God, and bringing into captivity every thought to the obedience of Christ; and having in a readiness to revenge all disobedience, when your obedience is fulfilled. (2 Corinthians 10:3–6)

Thus, it behooves us to get ready and stay armed with the Word of God so we can withstand the evil day. God has a plan for us to succeed. However, we must know and understand the plan so we can stay focused and obtain the victory that rightfully belongs to us! Jeremiah shares with us the Word of the Lord, "For I know the thoughts that I think toward you, saith the LORD, thoughts of peace, and not of evil, to give you an expected end" (Jeremiah 29:11).

In recent history, the global pandemic of 2019 brought international culture to a new awareness that life as we once knew it is gone. Disease and disasters have resulted in enormous loss of lives. Worldwide, there are wars and rumors of wars, riots, demonstrations, rallies, and so many other events orchestrated for destruction. In addition, in many places around the world, blatant racism and gross social injustices are on the rise. In this hour, there is widespread moral corruption as the worldwide media commonly reports on pastors, business leaders, leaders of countries, and even high-ranking royals with noble titles who are beginning to fail and be exposed as they walk in lives of duality.

Across the board, in all walks of life and cultures, the world's standard is moving more and more to the acceptance (and almost endorsement) of speaking one thing and doing another. As some describe these behaviors as "not walking their talk," the incipient progression of moral decline is reaching epic proportions in all areas of society.

In my doctoral dissertation, I wrote this, and it bears repeating here: "People working on the front lines in health care, departments of public safety, psychiatric hospitals, neuro-medical centers, nursing homes, and all essential workers are to be applauded. Good police officers, world leaders, and state and local officials are expected to do something to eradicate this problem. Still, the reality is that it is out of their control—God is in control!"

Yes, so it is that things are rapidly changing, but those who have discernment from God can see what is happening! These events are but a foretaste of what is to come as we get closer to the end of time. Interestingly, the earliest disciples of Jesus Christ also knew these feelings of instability and insecurity even in their age, as reflected in the Bible:

> And as he sat upon the Mount of Olives, the disciples came unto him privately, saying, "Tell us, when shall these things be? And what shall be the sign of thy coming and of the end of the world?" And Jesus answered and said unto them, "Take heed that no man deceive you. For many shall come in my name, saying, 'I am Christ,' and shall deceive many. *And ye shall hear of wars and rumours of wars: see that ye be not troubled: for all these things must come to pass, but the end is not yet.* For nation shall rise against nation, and kingdom against kingdom: and there shall be famines, and pestilences, and earthquakes, in divers places. All these are

the beginning of sorrows." (Matthew 24:3–8; emphasis added)

Yes, we recognize that there must be a separation between the redeemed person and the world. We cannot partake of their table and expect our actions to be acceptable to God. Faith pleases God. Faith works by Love. Love obeys. God requires that we follow his commandments, but He has also provided us with the power to do so. God gives us the power to live holy, consecrated lives. He equips us and helps us all the way with Scriptures like these below (and others):

> Now therefore, if ye will obey my voice indeed, and keep my covenant, then ye shall be a peculiar treasure unto me above all people: for all the earth is mine: and ye shall be unto me a kingdom of priests, and an holy nation. These are the words which thou shalt speak unto the children of Israel. (Exodus 19: 5–6)

> Ye adulterers and adulteresses, know ye not that the friendship of the world is enmity with God? Whosoever therefore will be a friend of the world is the enemy of God. Do ye think that the scripture saith in vain, The spirit that dwelleth in us lusteth to envy? But he giveth more grace. Wherefore he saith, God resisteth the proud, but giveth grace unto the humble.

Submit yourselves therefore to God. Resist the devil, and he will flee from you. Draw nigh to God, and he will draw nigh to you. Cleanse your hands, ye sinners; and purify your hearts, ye double minded. Be afflicted, and mourn, and weep: let your laughter **be turned to mourning, and your joy to heaviness.** Humble yourselves in the sight of the Lord, and he shall lift you up. (James 4: 4–10; emphasis added)

But as he which hath called you is holy, so be ye holy in all manner of conversation; Because it is written, Be ye holy; for I am holy. (1 Peter 1:15–16)

But ye are a chosen generation, a royal priesthood, an holy nation, a peculiar people; that ye should shew forth the praises of him who hath called you out of darkness into his marvellous light: Which in time past were not a people, but are now the people of God: which had not obtained mercy, but now have obtained mercy. (1 Peter 2:9–10)

For the sake of the Church, we must believe, receive, and truly know that we are indeed a chosen generation, a royal priesthood, a holy nation, a peculiar people (1 Peter 2:9). We must run this race with patience (Hebrews 12), be steadfast, unmovable, always abounding in the work of the Lord, forasmuch as you (we) know that your (our) labor is not in vain in the Lord (1 Corinthians 15:58).

CHAPTER ONE

The Church Defined

Most often, people think of a church as a building or perhaps a specific denomination of believers. Merriam-Webster defines the word church as "a building for public and especially Christian worship; the clergy or officialdom of a religious body; a body or organization of religious believers: such as the whole body of Christians."[1] Therefore, from the primary definition, we can understand that many words are synonymous with a church as a building, including words such as a synagogue, tabernacle, and temple.

Given that initial and natural definition, devoting this whole chapter to defining the church may seem basic or menial. But as we begin to think about and prioritize the meaning of the word *church* in the spiritual realm, we discover a dramatic and historical shift that signals the change of the spiritual season!

Interestingly, Jesus was the first person in the New Testament to use the term *church*. We find that he was no longer referring to a building or edifice made with hands. Instead, he employed the Greek word that identified the Church as a Body of Believers. This first use is found in Matthew 16:18, as Jesus was conversing with Peter (one of the twelve disciples/apostles). He said, "And I say also unto thee, that thou art Peter, and upon this rock I will build *my church;* and the gates of hell shall not prevail against it" (emphasis added).

The word *church* used in Matthew 16:18 is the Greek word "ekklēsía, ek-klay-see'-ah; from a compound of G1537 and a derivative of G2564; a calling out, i.e. (concretely) a popular meeting, especially a religious congregation (Jewish synagogue, or Christian community of members on earth or saints in heaven or both):—assembly, church."[2] We often see the modern spelling of the word as *ecclesia*, supporting the meaning of this chosen or called-out company.

> And when he had found him, he brought him unto Antioch. And it came to pass, that a whole year they assembled themselves with the church, and taught much people. And the disciples were called Christians first in Antioch. (Acts 11:26)

In the book of Acts, we find that the early church (chosen, called-out ones) met from house to house together and taught together for a whole year. It was these believers in Antioch that were the first to be referred to as Christians.

After the outpouring of the Holy Ghost, many people heard God's word and believed, and thousands were added to the church.

> Therefore let all the house of Israel know assuredly, that God hath made that same Jesus, whom ye have crucified, both Lord and Christ. Now when they heard this, they were pricked in their heart, and said unto Peter and to the rest of the apostles, Men and brethren, what shall we do?

> Then Peter said unto them, Repent, and be baptized every one of you in the name of Jesus Christ for the remission of sins, and ye shall receive the gift of the Holy Ghost.

> For the promise is unto you, and to your children, and to all that are afar off, even as many as the Lord our God shall call. And with many other words did he testify and exhort, saying, Save yourselves from this untoward generation. Then they that gladly received his word were baptized: and the same day there

were added unto them about three thousand souls. And they continued stedfastly in the apostles' doctrine and fellowship, and in breaking of bread, and in prayers. And fear came upon every soul: and many wonders and signs were done by the apostles. (Acts 2:36–42)

Again, notice that this references a group of believers. This passage makes one wonder why so many different opinions, denominations, and organizations arise to cause discord among the brethren (gender neutral) as it relates to the church. Perhaps it is because the church operates as two distinct bodies within one: an organization and an organism. We could think of it as an organism operating within an organization. However, it could still be confusing if we do not divide the word of God correctly.

The church functions as an organization that is based primarily on biblical principles. During His interactions with the disciples, Jesus spent little time in business affairs. However, He was a man of order. God did things in an orderly manner. He took His time to create heaven, earth, and man. Then, the Old Testament prophets did things in an orderly manner, and that custom continued throughout the Bible. Paul the apostle makes it clear in 1 Corinthians 14:40 that we should "Let all things be done decently and in order."

Jesus set the initial pattern for operating in excellence and order in Mark 12:17 (NKJV), where Jesus instructed them (and us) to " 'Render to Caesar the things that are Caesar's, and to God the things that are God's.' And they marveled at Him."

The Church as an Organization

With the birth of what we now know as the New Testament Church, we see in the Scripture that it became necessary to appoint *deacons* to take care of the administration of the church functions so that the apostles could continue to minister the Word. We see this essential appointment in several passages in the Book of Acts:

> They devoted themselves to the apostles' teaching and the fellowship, to the breaking of bread and the prayers. (Acts 2:42 ESV)

> And fear came upon every soul: and many wonders and signs were done by the apostles. And all that believed were together, and had all things common; and sold their possessions and goods, and parted them to all men, as every man had need. And they, continuing daily with one accord in the temple, and breaking bread from house to house, did eat their meat with gladness and singleness of heart, praising God, and having favour with all the people. And the Lord added to the church daily such as should be saved. (Acts 2:43–47)

And in those days, when the number of the disciples was multiplied, there arose a murmuring of the Grecians against the Hebrews, because their widows were neglected in the daily ministration. Then the twelve called the multitude of the disciples unto them, and said, It is not reason that we should leave the word of God, and serve tables. Wherefore, brethren, look ye out among you seven men of *honest report, full of the Holy Ghost and wisdom, whom we may appoint over this business. But we will give ourselves continually to prayer, and to the ministry of the word.* (Acts 6:1–4; emphasis added.)

Before flying past that on to the next thought, let's establish and acknowledge the power in those last two sentences! Honest men, full of the Holy Ghost and wisdom, are *still* needed *for the sake of the Church* to give themselves continually to prayer and the ministry of the Word!

The word used for deacon is the Greek word "diakonéō, dee-ak-on-eh'-o; from G1249; to be an attendant, i.e. wait upon (menially or as a host, friend, or (figuratively) teacher); technically, to act as a Christian deacon:—(ad-)minister (unto), serve, use the office of a deacon."[3]

The question to explore is, "What type of business did the deacons do?" The Biblical outline of usage tells us that to be a deacon is to be a servant, attendant, domestic, to serve, wait upon; to minister to one, render ministering offices to; to be served, ministered unto, to wait tables and offer food and drink to the guests. The same term was used for preparing food or the supply of food and necessities of life; to relieve one's necessities (e.g., by collecting alms), to provide, take care of, and distribute the things necessary to sustain life; to take care of the poor and the sick. The term was used for those who administer the office of a deacon in Christian churches, attending to anything that may serve another's interests.[4]

The bottom line is that the very essence of the work (or business) of a deacon is *serving*.

When the Grecians were murmuring against the Hebrews because their widows were being neglected in the daily ministration (food distribution), deacons were appointed to ensure fairness in support of all of the widows. The Lord led the apostles to appoint deacons who were graced for the work, and the work at that time was to make sure all of the widows were equally served! It wasn't preaching; it wasn't overseeing the apostles or pastors; it wasn't a political position nor a seat of authority. It was a privilege to be of service.

We see in 1 Timothy 3:8–13 the distinct qualifications for deacons:

> Likewise, must the deacons be grave, not double-tongued, not given to much wine, not greedy of filthy lucre; holding the mystery of the faith in a pure conscience. And let these also first be proved; then let them use the office

of a deacon, being found blameless. Even so must their wives be grave, not slanderers, sober, faithful in all things. Let the deacons be the husbands of one wife, ruling their children and their own houses well.

For they that have used the office of a deacon well purchase to themselves a good degree, and great boldness in the faith which is in Christ Jesus.

In 1 Timothy 5:3–7, the text identifies those who are considered widows and how the Church was expected to meet their needs:

Honour widows that are widows indeed. But if any widow have children or nephews, let them learn first to shew piety at home, and to requite their parents: for that is good and acceptable before God.

Now she that is a widow indeed, and desolate, trusteth in God, and continueth in supplications and prayers night and day.

But she that liveth in pleasure is dead while she liveth. And these things give in charge, that they may be blameless.

In Acts 4:32–37, we learn how the deacons obtained funds to take care of the people:

> And the multitude of them that believed were of one heart and of one soul: neither said any of them that ought of the things which he possessed was his own; but they had all things common.

> And with great power gave the apostles witness of the resurrection of the Lord Jesus: and great grace was upon them all. Neither was there any among them that lacked: for as many as were possessors of lands or houses sold them, and brought the prices of the things that were sold, and laid them down at the apostles' feet: and distribution was made unto every man according as he had need.

> And Joses, who by the apostles was surnamed Barnabas, (which is, being interpreted, The son of consolation,) a Levite, and of the country of Cyprus, having land, sold it, and brought the money, and laid it at the apostles' feet.

The Bible teaches us in this multitude of verses that we each have an obligation to grace *to provide for our own as much as possible*. Then, the church (made up of pastors, people, deacons, and others) has a responsibility to provide for those who are "widows indeed."

The simple meaning of that phrase is that where there are family members (the Bible mentions children and even nephews specifically) who should provide for the widow, the Lord expects that they shall do so thoroughly and in excellence as unto Him, or if the widow remarries, then that shall be her provision as from the Lord. But, if there are none, the church shall indeed provide for her care. So, with an understanding of the Scripture, we can recognize that it is an essential job that those deacons undertook, *and so it is today.*

In fact, in our defining the Church, we must also bring forward that *every position in the church is significant, every person important.* Every joint is rightly fitted and serves a specific purpose. This truth is vital in our defining of the Church and our observation that the Church is both an organization and a living organism.

Just recently, I heard Apostle Michael Artis preaching on the importance of every job in the church, as well as every member of the Body of Christ. To paint a mental picture, he drew on the essential roles of both the pastor and the custodian. Apostle Artis' probing question remains with me long after I heard the message. He asked, "Who wants to come into a dirty church to hear a clean message?" *Each role will impact the ability of the hearer to receive.* That simple example lets us know that the preacher is essential, but so is the custodian! Both are serving God, and both are contributing to the service of the Gospel without distraction. (And both must be clean and holy!)

As we continue to define the Church, we may observe that many guidelines and expectations have changed since the early church began. However, there are some procedures, principles, and patterns of behavior that the Bible says must remain stable, in place, and consistent. Let's examine some of those things in the remainder of this chapter.

Stewardship of the Church

Whether it is in giving and tithing, seed time and harvest, or the way of God's Kingdom and the lifestyle of the Believer, God would not have us ignorant concerning anything that relates to Him. Finances are no exception to this.

It's often easy for people to understand the need for order and accountability within any business or other public organization because of those appointed to handle other people's money. But over the decades and centuries, the Church has struggled to see itself in this light. We all know that it is not always easy for everyone to give freely, especially to tithe (give the ten percent), and this continues to be a controversial subject among many Christians. Some wonder if they should or must give tithes, asking themselves, "What if others don't give? What if the leadership doesn't give?" Or perhaps they ask, "Where is it written that one should tithe?" Or even "What is the tithe?" In all things—especially in financial matters—we see it is common for humanity to "strain out the gnat and swallow a camel" (Matthew 23:23–24) as they look for excuses to hold onto God's money, even after He tells us that *the love of money is a root of all evil.*

First, *we learn to give for godly reasons.* Our giving to God should be cultivated as a lifestyle because we want to honor God with a portion of our blessings—the blessings that we are acknowledging that He supplied! Listen, we can't beat Him giving, for when we give generously, He gives us more! The Bible says in 2 Corinthians 9:10–11 (AMP),

> Now He who provides seed for the sower and bread for food will provide and multiply your seed for sowing [that is, your resources] and increase the harvest of your righteousness [which shows itself in active goodness, kindness, and love]. You will be enriched in every way so that you may be generous, and this [generosity, administered] through us is producing thanksgiving to God [from those who benefit].

Through personal experiences, I can say that tithing is rewarding and that we can't become disgruntled and try to figure out every Scripture with our minds, for everything is not written—the Holy Spirit must also lead one. I have seen our finances build. Still, at other times, I have also seen them leaving so fast that my husband and I began to question what was happening to us! Our answer came through the Word of God and prophecy: *pay your tithes.*

Now, having seen God's faithfulness and having learned more of the Word on giving over the years, it is our joy to pay tithes, give offerings above the tithe, and give to others—*more than is required.* The important lesson as we grow and mature in the offerings of the Lord is that we must let the Lord direct our path! We cannot afford to risk anything hindering us from obeying our Lord and Savior, Jesus Christ. So, as it relates to tithing, let me share these scriptures with you:

> Woe to you, scribes and Pharisees, hypocrites! For you tithe mint and dill and cumin, and have neglected the weightier matters of the law: justice and mercy and faithfulness. *These you ought to have done, without neglecting the others.* You blind guides, straining out a gnat and swallowing a camel! Woe to you, scribes and Pharisees, hypocrites! For you clean the outside of the cup and the plate, but inside they are full of greed and self-indulgence. You blind Pharisee! First clean the inside of the cup and the plate, that the outside also may be clean. (Matthew 23:23–26 ESV; emphasis added)

It is often easy to see or to agree that we should pay the tithe of simple or small things (like the Pharisees did of the herbs, mint, anise, and cumin). Jesus teaches us that in doing so, we are not to omit the matters of law, judgment, mercy, and faith—all of these are important. Tithing and giving in judgment and faith deal not with tangible things but with us having the mind of Christ in all things. Cleaning the inside first teaches us that in all these issues and questions, *it is the heart that is at issue.*

Do you remember when Jesus told Peter to pay their taxes? As the King of kings, He didn't have to, but He wanted Caesar to have whatever belonged to him. Jesus set the example clearly:

> However, not to give offense to them, go to the sea and cast a hook and take the first fish that comes up, and when you open its mouth you will find a shekel. Take that and give it to them for me and for yourself. (Matthew 17:27 ESV)

Again, Jesus was not required to pay tribute, but He did so that He wouldn't offend them. He was setting an example for us. I would rather pay tithes than stand before Jesus and hear Him say that I should have but didn't. I don't want to take a chance on sacrificing the blessing on my household over ten percent of a dollar! Again, it is an issue of the heart. I trust God to bring in more than enough and plenty to give so we can actually give more than ten percent because God blesses us with abundance. If we give freely, we will receive from so many different channels—we have One source, but He uses many channels!

The first real question is, "Do you trust God enough to let go of tithes and offerings—which come from that which He blessed you with first—and depend on Him to supply all your needs? Do you know that we have His promise to do so? "But my God shall supply all your need according to his riches in glory by Christ Jesus" (Philippians 4:19).

Some other questions to ask ourselves during reflection might be, "Are my ways pleasing to my Savior/Keeper?" Hebrews 11:6 tells us,

> And without faith it is impossible to please him, for *whoever would draw near to God must believe that He exists and that He rewards those who seek Him.* (ESV; emphasis added)

Or, for some of you, the first question might be, "Does my income seem to almost vanish before my eyes?" And second, "Does it appear that the more I work, the less I have?" We can find answers to possible reasons and remedies in the Word of God! Like what we see in Haggai, for instance. Let's take a look at that next.

> Now therefore thus saith the Lord of hosts; "*Consider your ways.* Ye have sown much, and bring in little; ye eat, but ye have not enough; ye drink, but ye are not filled with drink; ye clothe you, but there is none warm; and he that earneth wages earneth wages to put it into a bag with holes."

> Thus saith the Lord of hosts; "Consider your ways. Go up to the mountain, and bring wood,

and build the house; and I will take pleasure in it, and I will be glorified, saith the Lord. Ye looked for much, and, lo, it came to little; and when ye brought it home, I did blow upon it. Why?" saith the Lord of hosts.

"Because of mine house that is waste, and ye run every man unto his own house. Therefore the heaven over you is stayed from dew, and the earth is stayed from her fruit. And I called for a drought upon the land, and upon the mountains, and upon the corn, and upon the new wine, and upon the oil, and upon that which the ground bringeth forth, and upon men, and upon cattle, and upon all the labour of the hands."

Then Zerubbabel the son of Shealtiel, and Joshua the son of Josedech, the high priest, with all the remnant of the people, *obeyed the voice of the Lord their God*, and the words of Haggai the prophet, as the Lord their God had sent him, and the people did fear before the Lord. (Haggai 1:5–12; emphasis added)

Consider your ways. Are they the ways of the Lord? Ask yourself the hard questions. *Do you agree with God in your actions?* Throughout the ages, there have been many sinners who have tithed faithfully to their religious organizations. Tithing won't get any one of them into Heaven, but they will receive righteous judgment for their sacrifice, as do the children of God. Tithing isn't about your salvation but rather is *an act of obedience in response to the grace you have been given.*

> All things come alike to all: there is one event to the righteous, and to the wicked; to the good and to the clean, and to the unclean; to him that sacrificeth, and to him that sacrificeth not: as is the good, so is the sinner; and he that sweareth, as he that feareth an oath. (Ecclesiastes 9:2)

> Give…it shall be given unto you; good measure, pressed down, and shaken together, and running over, shall men give into your bosom. For with the same measure that ye mete withal, it shall be measured to you again. (Luke 6:38)

We see in these verses that in the manner we give, it shall also be given unto us. It is the Lord's promise and a Kingdom principle. The key word is *give*. Now, let's look again at that passage in Luke 6:38 to identify *what* we *receive* when we give *with the right attitude*:

> Good measure, pressed down, and shaken together, and running over, shall men give into

17

your bosom. For with the same measure that ye
mete withal, it shall be measured to you again.

This passage literally means *you place yourself in the position
to receive* too much for the container or the storehouse! Whatever you sow will return to you, but it does not necessarily
return as money. Sometimes, we feel that our blessings must
come in the form of cash, but rest assured that having favor, a
good family, good health, food, security, and a decent place to
live are worth so much more than cash. Humanity as a whole
tends to take so many things for granted! It is so common in
modern cultures to take for granted our daily blessings (large
or small) that we don't even acknowledge the blessings until
suddenly we no longer have them. **Our giving serves to loosen
the grip of covetousness from its hold on our hearts, and
gratitude helps us to intersect the provision of God, recognize it, and receive it when it arrives!**

In Ecclesiastes 11:1, the Scripture tells us to "Cast thy
bread upon the waters: for thou shalt find it after many days."
This principle teaches us obedience to the grace that has been
shown and given to us. God is a forgiving God who has given
us opportunity after opportunity to be obedient to his commandments. Yet, **people continue to disobey and miss the
opportunities to prosper because they will not deny themselves to honor God and to minister help to others**.

And the Spirit of God came upon Zechariah, the
son of Jehoiada the priest, which stood above

the people, and said unto them, Thus saith God, Why transgress ye the commandments of the LORD, *that ye cannot prosper?* Because ye have forsaken the LORD, he hath also forsaken you. (2 Chronicles 24:20; emphasis added.)

For I am the LORD, I change not; therefore ye sons of Jacob are not consumed. Even from the days of your fathers ye are gone away from mine ordinances, and have not kept them. Return unto me, and I will return unto you, saith the LORD of hosts. But ye said, "Wherein shall we return?" Will a man rob God? **Yet ye have robbed me**. But ye say, *"Wherein have we robbed thee?"* **In tithes and offerings**. Ye are cursed with a curse: for ye have robbed me, even this whole nation. (Malachi 3:6–9; emphasis added)

These passages tell us how we rob God—in tithes and of-ferings. Which of you desire to be cursed with a curse, not by man, but by God? Not me. The great news is that God tells us how to avoid the curse!

Bring ye all the tithes into the storehouse, that there may be meat in mine house, and prove me now herewith, saith the LORD of hosts, if I will not open you the windows of heaven, and

19

pour you out a blessing, that there shall not be room enough to receive it. *And I will rebuke the devourer for your sakes*, and he shall not destroy the fruits of your ground; neither shall your vine cast her fruit before the time in the field, saith the LORD of host. And all nations shall call you blessed: for ye shall be a delightsome land, saith the LORD of hosts. (Malachi 3:10–12; emphasis added)

Bring *all* the tithes *to the storehouse* (and bring the offerings according to His Word); not only will you receive abundant blessings, but He will rebuke the devourer for your sake! These verses have enough promises to convince me that tithing is in my best interest! Clearly, we see that tithing not only brings meat into the storehouse (provision for the things of the Lord in the Church), but God rebukes the devourer for our sakes (the tithers), **resulting in a blessing that there shall not be room enough to receive it**. That is exciting! God makes it abundantly clear to those who have ears to hear and eyes to see, written in 2 Corinthians 9:6–15:

The point is this: whoever sows sparingly will also reap sparingly, and whoever sows bountifully will also reap bountifully. Each one must give *as he has decided in his heart, not reluctantly or under compulsion*, for **God loves a cheerful giver**. And God is able to make all grace abound to you, so that *having all sufficiency in all things at all times*, you may abound in every good work. As it is written, "He has distributed freely, he has given to the poor; his righteousness endures forever."

He who supplies seed to the sower and bread for food will supply and multiply your seed for sowing and increase the harvest of your righteousness. You will be enriched in every way to be generous in every way, which through us will produce thanksgiving to God.

For the ministry of this service is not only supplying the needs of the saints but is also overflowing in many thanksgivings to God. By their approval of this service, they will glorify God because of your submission that comes from your confession of the gospel of Christ, and the generosity of your contribution for them and for all others, while they long for you and pray for you, because of the surpassing grace of God upon you. Thanks be to God for his inexpressible gift. (ESV; emphasis added)

Notice the emphasis on sowing and reaping, which is "as he has decided in his heart, not reluctantly or under compulsion." We also notice the blessing in giving and how it increases the fruit of one's righteousness, supplying not only the needs but some of the wants of the giver and all those around them! Today, we see small churches with a few members, mega-churches with thousands of members, and international and television ministries that all require basic order for business.

While the church is expected to meet the spiritual needs of the people through its leadership, it also takes unity and knowledge to meet the financial obligations of the church. These tithes, offerings, and administrations thereof are both Biblical and required to ensure staff is compensated (as a worker is worth their wages), that utilities, maintenance, and other functions are funded and performed, and that local and federal laws are enforced. So, one can realize that there is a legitimate need for administration as well as legal and corporate functions. Effective leadership and organization is vital for the church to function as our Lord intended.

So, where is the disconnect? Where have the problems come in? Any number of things may have an impact. Lack of teaching of the Word is a primary cause, which is why I felt compelled to include this teaching *for the sake of the Church*. Other considerations could be when sin, division, competition, and complacency enter the heart of the believer(s). Spiritual weakness on behalf of the leader, traditions of men or even false teachings, and the Church forgetting its first love—Christ—are all reasons to expect that people will cease to tithe and give. If these things continue, eventually, that local church will fail to meet its operation expenses and be forced to close, sell, or cease to serve the community.

Please don't misunderstand. Our God always has somebody ready, willing, and able to stand in the breech for His people, the Church, and to plead for the souls of the unsaved! Like Mordecai told Esther (in Esther 4:12–14), rescue will arise from another place! Therefore, *for the sake of the Church, God will raise a remnant that will survive and thrive!* Jesus' words will never lose their power, and He said that the gates of hell would not prevail against His Church! But those who were assigned in the first place to bring into that storehouse will forfeit the rewards they might otherwise have experienced. The reward of the Lord should be highly esteemed, and the gravity of that loss to those who forfeit the reward should not be underestimated.

The Church as a Living Organ

Now, let's look at the church as an *organism* rather than just an organization. According to the Merriam-Webster Dictionary, an *organism* is a noun meaning "a complex structure of interdependent and subordinate elements whose relations and properties are largely determined *by their function* in the whole."[5] A second and appropriate definition is "an individual constituted to carry on the activities of life by means of parts or organs more or less separate in function but mutually dependent: a living being."

Thus, we see the Church as an *organism*—a single being with many separate parts, each with its particular function; the organism cannot survive without the parts, as the parts cannot survive without the organism—this is a description of the corporate Body of Christ, the Church. Therefore, the church must recognize its identity as a Body, with many members operating independently yet connectively. As a living, functional entity on earth, each member is required to work according to the will of God, always remembering that we cannot do anything without the Head, Jesus Christ.

Paul wrote of the Body this way in 1 Corinthians 12:12–18, 25–27 (MSG; emphasis added):

> You can easily enough see how this kind of thing works by looking no further than your own body. Your body has many parts—limbs, organs, cells—but no matter how many parts you can name, you're still one body. It's exactly the same with Christ.

> By means of his one Spirit, we all said good-bye to our partial and piecemeal lives. We each used to independently call our own shots, but then we entered into a large and integrated life in which he has the final say in everything. (This is what we proclaimed in word and action when we were baptized.) Each of us is now a part of his resurrection body, refreshed and sustained at one fountain—his Spirit—where we all come to drink. The old labels we once used to identify ourselves—labels like Jew or Greek, slave or free—are no longer useful. We need something larger, more comprehensive.

I want you to think about how all this makes you more significant, not less. A body isn't just a single part blown up into something huge. It's all the different-but-similar parts arranged and functioning together. If Foot said, "I'm not elegant like Hand, embellished with rings; I guess I don't belong to this body," would that make it so? If Ear said, "I'm not beautiful like Eye, limpid and expressive; I don't deserve a place on the head," would you want to remove it from the body? If the body was all eye, how could it hear? If all ear, how could it smell? As it is, we see that God has carefully placed each part of the body right where he wanted it.

The way God designed our bodies is a model for understanding our lives together as a church: every part dependent on every other part, the parts we mention and the parts we don't, the parts we see and the parts we don't. If one part hurts, every other part is involved in the hurt, and the healing. If one part flourishes, every other part enters into the exuberance. You are Christ's body—that's who you are! You must never forget this. Only as you accept your part of that body does your "part" mean anything.

The Scripture helps us understand how we are connected and why believers in Christ are called the Body of Christ—a living organism! As such, the organism thrives with specific nourishment and provision. For example, prayer is as essential to the Body of Christ as oxygen is to the human body! If you don't believe this, check with someone who has asthma or some form of chronic lung disease. Sometimes, they have to speak into the atmosphere that all the air belongs to our God and thank Him for every breath of air before they get relief when they have an attack. So it is true that the spiritual being that is the Body of Christ, individually and corporately, cannot survive without effective, fervent prayer—we cannot thrive without communion and communication with our Creator and giver of life.

According to James 5:16 (ESV; emphasis added), we are to "confess [our] sins to one another and pray for one another, **that [we] may be healed**. The prayer of a righteous person has great power as it is working." Other translations say that "the effective, fervent prayer of a righteous man availeth much." Thus, we confirm in the Word that confession and forgiveness of sins, as well as praying for one another, all contribute to the health, healing, and life of the organism.

In the next several passages of Scripture from John 17:9–12, 20–23, we see that Jesus prayed for those He had received, that through salvation they would be given eternal *life*. Look at the passion with which He prayed that they be one with His Father:

I pray for them: I pray not for the world, but for them which thou hast given me; for they are thine. And all mine are thine, and thine are mine; and I am glorified in them. And now I am no more in the world, but these are in the world, and I come to thee. Holy Father, keep through thine own name those whom thou hast given me, that they may be one, as we are. While I was with them in the world, I kept them in thy name: those that thou gavest me I have kept, and none of them is lost, but the son of perdition; that the Scripture might be fulfilled.

Neither pray I for these alone, but for them also which shall believe on me through their word; that they all may be one; as thou, Father, art in me, and I in thee, that they also may be one in us: that the world may believe that thou hast sent me.

And the glory which thou gavest me I have given them; that they may be one, even as we are one: I in them, and thou in me, that they may be made perfect in one; and that the world may know that thou hast sent me, and hast loved them, as thou hast loved me.

So, the life of the organism comes from that communion, being one in Christ. That communion is expressed in part as *prayer*. The Church must have a corporate prayer life. Now, just saying words or calling on the Lord when trouble comes is not necessarily prayer. Praying is a part of the Church's whole life-giving *lifestyle*. Prayer is the Believer's channel of communication that provides access to our Heavenly Father based on our relationship with His Son, Jesus Christ. We can have confidence when we pray in faith that God hears the cries and prayers of His children. And He answers those prayers.

We can look at the lives of Elijah and Daniel, whom the Bible identifies as men who were known for having lifestyles of prayer, and it also tells us of God's answers to those prayers. We see that the prophet Elijah was a man who prayed fervently and effectively, and God answered his faith-filled, powerful prayers.

> Elias was a man subject to like passions as we are, and he prayed earnestly that it might not rain: and it rained not on the earth by the space of three years and six months. And he prayed again, and the heaven gave rain, and the earth brought forth her fruit. (James 5:17–18)

Likewise, Daniel was a man of prayer. We see the story in Daniel, Chapter 6, where he refused to fall down and worship the King's royal stature, knowing that the punishment for refusing would mean he would be cast into the den of lions. Rather than obey the King, Daniel openly and faithfully prayed to his

God three times a day. He knew God would deliver him, and God did just that because Daniel prayed and believed his God!

It's more than just praying *or* believing. These two things function together. You must pray and believe. You must believe and pray. Here is the rest of the story in Daniel 6:19–23 (emphasis added):

> Then the king arose very early in the morning, and went in haste unto the den of lions. And when he came to the den, he cried with a lamentable voice unto Daniel: and the king spake and said to Daniel, "O Daniel, servant of the living God, is thy God, whom thou servest continually, able to deliver thee from the lions?"

> Then said Daniel unto the king, "O king, live for ever. My God hath sent his angel, and hath shut the lions' mouths, that they have not hurt me: forasmuch as before him innocency was found in me; and also before thee, O king, have I done no hurt."

> Then was the king exceedingly glad for him, and commanded that they should take Daniel up out of the den. So Daniel was taken up out of the den, and no manner of hurt was found upon him, **because he believed in his God**.

Wow! Look at the mighty power of God toward one who trusted Him! It was definitely faith that took Daniel through that trial. It just amazes me that the lions consumed those accusers, their children, and their wives before they ever got to the bottom of the den. This is further proof that effective prayer—fervent prayer—works!

When we study the New Testament, we find many times when Jesus prayed and how He taught others (and us) to pray. In Matthew 6:5–13, He spoke with his disciples directly about prayer:

> And when thou prayest, thou shalt not be as the hypocrites are: for they love to pray standing in the synagogues and in the corners of the streets, that they may be seen of men. Verily I say unto you, They have their reward. But thou, when thou prayest, enter into thy closet, and when thou hast shut thy door, pray to thy Father which is in secret; and thy Father which seeth in secret shall reward thee openly.
>
> But when ye pray, use not vain repetitions, as the heathen do: for they think that they shall be heard for their much speaking. Be not ye therefore like unto them: for your Father knoweth what things ye have need of, before ye ask him.

After this manner therefore pray ye: Our
Father which art in heaven, Hallowed be thy
name. Thy kingdom come. Thy will be done
in earth, as it is in heaven. Give us this day
our daily bread. And forgive us our debts, as
we forgive our debtors. And lead us not into
temptation, but deliver us from evil: For thine
is the kingdom, and the power, and the glory,
for ever. Amen

Life becomes simple when we realize that God created
everything and everything belongs to Him. Yes, indeed, the
Church is an organism, a living body of believers! The church
finds life in her identity as a living organism because:

Jesus Christ said, "I am the resurrection and
the life." (John 11:25)

And you hath he quickened [made alive], who
were dead in trespasses and sins. (Ephesians
2:1; emphasis added)

To whom He states, "I am the good shepherd:
the good shepherd giveth his life for the sheep."
(John 10:11)

God is the "I Am"—he is not the God of the dead, but
of the living (from Matthew 22:32). He is our God; we are

the people (sheep) of his pasture (from Psalm 95:7 and Psalm 100:3).

Jesus lived, died, and arose *for the sake of the Church!* Jesus lives, and because He lives, we also live. Hallelujah! God lives in us, and He is the head of the Body, which is the Church. We can do nothing without Him. He is the very essence of our life. What a glorious promise that, as a living part of His Body, the corporate Body of Christ, we will never die!

Oh yes, we will sleep in Him for a time, but John 11:25 tells us that he that believeth (that's you and me) in Jesus shall never die. You see, there will be a transition when we shall all be changed. It will happen in a moment, in the twinkling of an eye, at the last trump: for the trumpet shall sound, and the dead (those who slept away in Christ) shall be raised incorruptible. We shall be changed! That is all in 1 Corinthians 15:51–52. The Bible also says,

> Then we which are alive and remain shall be caught up together with them in the clouds, to meet the Lord in the air: and so shall we ever be with the Lord. Wherefore comfort one another with these words. (1 Thessalonian 4:17–18)

We must remember that these promises are **to the ones who are saved** (as Apostle Michael Artis says, "saved to the bone"), born-again Christians—the Church. We must also re-member that "the Son of man is come to seek and to save that which was lost" (Luke 19:10).

32

> For God sent not his Son into the world to condemn the world; but that the world through him might be saved. He that believeth on him is not condemned: but he that believeth not is condemned already, because he hath not believed in the name of the only begotten Son of God. (John 3:17–18)

As believers in Christ, we can be strengthened by knowing that Jesus is the Chief Cornerstone of the church.

> And He Himself existed and is before all things, and in Him all things hold together. [His is the controlling, cohesive force of the universe.] He is also the head [the life-source and leader] of the body, the church; and He is the beginning, the firstborn from the dead, so that He Himself will occupy the first place [He will stand supreme and be preeminent] in everything.

> For it pleased the Father for all the fullness [of deity—the sum total of His essence, all His perfection, powers, and attributes] to dwell [permanently] in Him (the Son), and through [the intervention of] the Son to reconcile all things to Himself, making peace [with believers] through the blood of His cross; through Him,

[I say,] whether things on earth or things in heaven. (Colossians 1:17–20 AMP)

Further, three books in the Bible (Matthew, Mark, and Luke) tell us that heaven and earth shall pass away, but His Word will forever stand. The Gospel of John declares,

> In the beginning was the Word, and the Word was with God, and the Word was God. (John 1:1)

> And the Word was made flesh, and dwelt among us, (and we beheld his glory, the glory as of the only begotten of the Father,) full of grace and truth. (John 1:14)

This is how we can rejoice and be fully assured that Jesus is the Word. Hallelujah to the King of Kings and Lord of Lords! And *for the sake of the Church*, He will never pass away.

Chapter Two

The Greatest Sacrifice

Greater love hath no man than this, that a man
lay down his life for his friends. (John 15:13)

What a great honor it is to be called a friend of God! We
are beyond blessed that Jesus calls us his friends. Isn't it amaz-
ing that we go from being his enemy to being his friends? He
even elevates us from being servants who do not know what
their Lord is doing to being his friends because he has made
known to us the things he heard of his Father. As a matter of
fact, Jesus loved us so much that he prayed for us! And the only
thing required of us is to do whatever he commands us, and his
commandments are not grievous.

As we grow and mature in the Word of God, we come to
know that there is a difference between worldly friends and the

forever friend that we have in Jesus. He will never leave us or forsake us, and in fulfilling His mission, His goal is to keep us. Jesus teaches us through His Word and His actions that a true godly friend will think nothing at all of being inconvenienced so he can help a friend! Sharing, caring, and denying self are all a part of a true friendship.

In all of our lives, we encounter those who say they are friends, but in times of need, they cannot be found or bothered. Sadly, we learn through disappointments not to put their friendship to the test of an extraordinary request. On the other hand, I am thankful to have friends who I can call on in my time of need, and they will help me and stand firmly in faith with me! Friends like my prayer partners, Minister Oates, Minister J. Williams, Mother B. Barnes, Brother and Sister Patterson, Sisters Teresa and Mary, Brother Xavier, and others whom I can call on. (These are but a few close ones. I'm so thankful to God that I actually have so many that I can't name them all here!)

An excellent example of a faithful and true friend is my prayer partner and sister-in-law, Minister Williams, who spent numerous hours several times each week in the car with me as I waited for my husband to have his prescribed medical treatment. I'm speaking of great inconvenience, four to five hours at a time, three times a week in the North Carolina summer heat!

Jesus is our pattern for true friendship. We must have that sacrificial type of relationship with our friends! Many times, the need will be at the dawn of the day or late in the midnight hour, yet people need you when they need you! My husband

and I, along with a few friends, have traveled miles to show our love and support for friends going through tough times or sickness. In other words, we had to make sacrifices to fulfill God's mission for us. *For the sake of the Church*, the Church must arise in this practice of *becoming excellent friends*, being reliable, showing up for one another, and helping one another remain steady in times of challenge. This is especially true for those in the five-fold ministry; we are held to a higher standard, an excellent love walk.

True prophets, pastors, and witnesses are charged with activating the word of God, living holy, and faithfully proclaiming to mankind that you must be born again. Remember our exhortation from earlier? *Consider your ways.*

It's time to give up the sinful pleasures of this world, including selfishness and disloyalty. It's time to take an inventory of your life, behaviors, and attitudes. It's time to evaluate ourselves to see if we have any genuine love for others. Any patience? Any tolerance and grace for others? Are you willing to get up in the early morning before the dawn of the day to help your neighbor? When the phone rings after midnight, do you refuse to answer and simply say, "Lord have mercy!" Do you wonder in aggravation what they could want or who's calling this time of night? Or are you readily available to help and encourage at any hour?

We've got to get these little things that hinder our growth out of our lives. It's time for us to cry loud and spare not. Even in the Old Testament, we see that the prophets acknowledged sin as well as prophesying about the coming Messiah.

The Word of God in the book of Isaiah speaks of the coming Messiah's righteous reign:

> Then a Shoot (the Messiah) will spring from the stock of Jesse [David's father], And a Branch from his roots will bear fruit.
>
> And the Spirit of the Lord will rest on Him— The Spirit of wisdom and understanding, The Spirit of counsel and strength, The Spirit of knowledge and of the [reverential and obedient] fear of the Lord—and He will delight in the fear of the Lord, and He will not judge by what His eyes see, nor make decisions by what His ears hear; but with righteousness and justice He will judge the poor, and decide with fairness for the downtrodden of the earth; and He shall strike the earth with the rod of His mouth, and with the breath of His lips He shall slay the wicked.
>
> And righteousness will be the belt around His loins, and faithfulness the belt around His waist. Then in that day...The nations will make supplications to the Root of Jesse Who will stand as a signal for the peoples; and His resting place will be glorious. (Isaiah 11:1–5, 10–11 AMP)

Isaiah 53:2–12 (AMP) tells us not only of the coming Messiah but also of the sacrifice He would make to redeem mankind:

> For He [the Servant of God] grew up before Him like a tender shoot (plant), And like a root out of dry ground; He has no stately form or majestic splendor that we would look at Him, nor [handsome] appearance that we would be attracted to Him.
>
> He was despised and rejected by men, a Man of sorrows and pain and acquainted with grief; and like One from whom men hide their faces he was despised, and we did not appreciate His worth or esteem Him. But [in fact] He has borne our griefs, and He has carried our sorrows and pains; yet we [ignorantly] assumed that He was stricken, struck down by God and degraded and humiliated [by Him].
>
> But He was wounded for our transgressions, He was crushed for our wickedness [our sin, our injustice, our wrongdoing]; The punishment [required] for our well-being fell on Him, and by His stripes (wounds) we are healed.

All of us like sheep have gone astray, we have turned, each one, to his own way; but the Lord has caused the wickedness of us all [our sin, our injustice, our wrongdoing] to fall on Him [instead of us].

He was oppressed and He was afflicted, yet He did not open His mouth [to complain or defend Himself]; like a lamb that is led to the slaughter, and like a sheep that is silent before her shearers, so He did not open His mouth.

After oppression and judgment He was taken away; and as for His generation [His contemporaries], who [among them] concerned himself with the fact that He was cut off from the land of the living [by His death] for the transgression of my people, to whom the stroke [of death] was due?

His grave was assigned with the wicked, but He was with a rich man in His death, because He had done no violence, nor was there any deceit in His mouth. Yet the Lord was willing to crush Him, causing Him to suffer; if He would give Himself as a guilt offering [an atonement for sin], He shall see His [spiritual] offspring, He shall prolong His days, and the will (good pleasure) of the Lord shall succeed and prosper in His hand.

As a result of the anguish of His soul, He shall see it and be satisfied; by His knowledge [of what He has accomplished] the Righteous One, My Servant, shall justify the many [making them righteous—upright before God, in right standing with Him], for He shall bear [the responsibility for] their sins.

Therefore, I will divide and give Him a portion with the great [kings and rulers], and He shall divide the spoils with the mighty, because He [willingly] poured out His life to death, and was counted among the transgressors; yet He Himself bore and took away the sin of many, and interceded [with the Father] for the transgressors.

Although the Old Testament provides us with revelation and record of the law, we must keep in mind that the law was weak through the flesh, but "God sending his own Son in the likeness of sinful flesh, and for sin, condemned sin in the flesh" (Romans 8:3).

Jesus was born with an agenda given to him by His Father. He came to do His Father's will, to redeem mankind. Jesus interacted with all types of people, yet he remained faithful to

His mission. He performed miracles, fed thousands, and, most of all, brought salvation to the people.

We, too, have an agenda. If given a choice, most of us would gladly accept and partake of Jesus's miracles and goodness. But how many of us would sacrifice to be eligible for those benefits through the obedience of faith? And to the level that Jesus did?

We receive *benefits* from God just as we acknowledge and receive His *blessings*. Psalm 103:2–6 lists some of the benefits: He is the one who forgives; who gives health; who redeems; who crowns with righteousness; and who satisfies, so that your youth is renewed like the eagles'. The Bible tells us that the Lord executed righteousness and judgment *for all* who are oppressed.

Jesus lived in the world as a human being so he could identify with us on every level—infant, child, adult—yet he had no sin. He made the promise of even more benefits as He prepared to undertake the greatest sacrifice in our place. In the tenth chapter of John, we find a parable from Jesus that describes the good shepherd (Himself) who gives his life for the sheep. Jesus made a startling declaration when He revealed the power of His life and the love of His Father:

> I am the good shepherd, and know my sheep, and am known of mine. As the Father knoweth me, even so know I the Father: and I lay down my life for the sheep. And other sheep I have, which are not of this fold: them also I must bring, and they shall hear my voice; and there

shall be one fold, and one shepherd. Therefore doth my Father love me, because I lay down my life, that I might take it again. No man taketh it from me, but I lay it down of myself. I have power to lay it down, and I have power to take it again. This commandment have I received of my Father. (John 10:14–18)

If we can look beyond the surface with a spiritual eye, we will see that it wasn't just the sacrifice of giving His life for us (sinners) that is so remarkable. But, look at what Jesus endured, being denied by those who were closest to Him, living a life without sin and without yielding to the fleshly pleasures of the world, healing and forgiving people who would not forsake their traditions to follow Him. And then, at the apex of his life on earth, appeared before Pontius Pilate–the Roman governor of Judea who found no fault in Jesus–who unjustly released a notorious prisoner instead of Jesus. Rather than cause a tumult among the people that might be reported to Rome, he gave consent to the Jews for Jesus to be crucified.

Jesus did not have to take the bitter cup of crucifixion, but he endured it for the sake of the Church and made the greatest sacrifice for us. The Scriptures record the happenings that night Jesus was arrested and subsequently awaited crucifixion:

As Jesus was still speaking, Judas [Iscariot], one of the twelve [disciples], came up accompanied by a large crowd with swords and clubs, [who came as representatives] from the chief priests and elders of the people. Now the betrayer had given them a sign, saying, "Whomever I kiss, He is the one; seize Him." Immediately Judas went to Jesus and said, "Greetings (rejoice), Rabbi!" And he kissed Him [in a deliberate act of betrayal]. Jesus said to Judas, "Friend, do what you came for."

Then they came and seized Jesus and arrested Him. And one of those who were with Jesus reached out and drew his sword, and struck [Malchus] the slave of the high priest and cut off his ear. Then Jesus said to him, "Put your sword back in its place; for all those who habitually draw the sword will die by the sword. Do you think that I cannot appeal to My Father, and He will immediately provide Me with more than twelve legions of angels? How then will the Scriptures be fulfilled, that it must happen this way?"

At that moment Jesus said to the crowds, "Have you come out with swords and clubs to arrest Me as you would against a robber? Day after day I used to sit in the porches and courts of the temple teaching, and you did not arrest Me. But all this has taken place so that the

Scriptures of the prophets would be fulfilled."
Then all the disciples deserted Him and fled.
(Matthew 26:47–56 AMP)

And think of this: He died as the propitiation for our sins—and called us to receive the gift of salvation—while we were still yet sinners! Those who accept His payment for our sins and believe in Him as Lord and Savior become a part of the Body of Christ. Then, *you are no longer a sinner* but a saint—*a redeemed one.*

His promises that he would rise from the dead in three days and that he would send a Comforter, who is the Holy Ghost, have been fulfilled! That's what is so remarkable. Not only was he crucified, but he rose from the dead after three days, with all power in His hand! Glory to God! It all belongs to Him, the kingdom, the power, and the glory forever!

Yes, some may ask, "Wasn't Lazarus raised from the dead after three days (signifying that Jesus was not the only one raised from the dead)?" Lazarus was indeed raised from the dead. However, Jesus *called Lazarus to come forth.* Lazarus did not have the absolute power that Jesus was given. Lazarus died again later in life, as did others who were raised from the dead—except for Jesus. Jesus came alive because of His Father's plan for him. And He *ever lives* to intercede for us. He ever lives! Therefore, Jesus' resurrection was the fulfillment of prophecy, a step in the process of a master plan.

Because He is not slack concerning His promises, every promise he made is either fulfilled (through the prophets) or is in the process of being fulfilled (through the Church). We must continue to look for his promises, to be rooted, grounded, and adequately clothed in His Word so we can stand against the wiles of the devil. Ephesians 6:11–18 (ESV) teaches us to:

> Put on the whole armor of God, that you may be able to stand against the schemes of the devil. For we do not wrestle against flesh and blood, but against the rulers, against the authorities, against the cosmic powers over this present darkness, against the spiritual forces of evil in the heavenly places.
>
> Therefore take up the whole armor of God, that you may be able to withstand in the evil day, and having done all, to stand firm. Stand therefore, having fastened on the belt of truth, and having put on the breastplate of righteousness, and, as shoes for your feet, having put on the readiness given by the gospel of peace.
>
> In all circumstances take up the shield of faith, with which you can extinguish all the flaming darts of the evil one; and take the helmet of salvation, and the sword of the Spirit, which is the word of God, praying at all times in the Spirit, with all prayer and supplication. To that

end, keep alert with all perseverance, making supplication for all the saints.

And in 1 Peter 2:9–10 (ESV), the Word reiterates who we are as a result of receiving the gift of His mercy:

> But you are a chosen race, a royal priesthood, a holy nation, a people for his own possession, that you may proclaim the excellencies of him who called you out of darkness into his marvelous light. Once you were not a people, but now you are God's people; once you had not received mercy, but now you have received mercy.

We are blood-bought Christians! We are a chosen generation, a royal priesthood, a holy nation, a peculiar people. We are the people of God! Romans 12:1–2 instructs us how to respond to His lavish gift of life:

> Present your bodies as a living sacrifice, holy, acceptable unto God, which is your reasonable service. And be not conformed to this world: but be ye transformed by the renewing of your mind, that ye may prove what is that good, and acceptable, and perfect, will of God.

Notice in that previous verse (v. 2), we are to "be not conformed to this world." Conformity, in this instance, is dangerous. It can cause you to deceive yourself. Going along with the majority is not always the best solution for believers. On the other hand, transformation brings about a positive change. The result is that one follows the teachings and commandments of our Lord as written in the Scripture. Transformation is a process in our lives; we change daily to operate in the will of God. (That's why many often refer to themselves as a work in progress.)

Think about this: for whom would you give your life? We offer many things in the name of love (food, money, body parts, shelter), but our life is another consideration altogether! For whom would you sacrifice your life?

Now, let's think about the reality of life in the context of this description in James 4:13–17:

> Go to now, ye that say, To day or to morrow we will go into such a city, and continue there a year, and buy and sell, and get gain: Whereas ye know not what shall be on the morrow. For what is your life? It is even a vapour, that appeareth for a little time, and then vanisheth away. For that ye ought to say, "If the Lord will, we shall live, and do this, or that." But now ye rejoice in your boastings: all such rejoicing is evil. Therefore to him that knoweth to do good, and doeth it not, to him it is sin.

Life is so fragile and simple, but, on the other hand, it is also complicated! We really can't determine how to navigate all of our needs, desires, and problems on our own. But we can put our trust in the Lord!

Just recently, I had the opportunity to visit with a marvelous young lady named Yvette. As we talked, she began to share her testimony about life and living. Among other things, she shared the impact her grandmother has had on her life, encouraging her to be the best she can be in everything she does. (Yvette speaks of her grandmother, Ma, in the present, although she has been deceased for years.) She also told of how she is a twenty-two-year metastatic breast cancer survivor of not one but two different cancers. She's carrying her cross with a smile, a joyous spirit, and a love from God that radiates from her environment.

Speaking about the twenty-two-year journey, she said, "Who else could God have given to carry this breast cancer for twenty-two years? He chose me, and there's no one greater than me to do it. God lives in me! I am the BEST BREAST CANCER SURVIVOR!" I believe she is a sacrifice for many, showing us that God's got us, no matter what comes our way!

So, after all of your sacrifices, would they or could they give the recipient eternal life? Jesus provides us with the most thought-provoking question regarding this subject:

> Then said Jesus unto his disciples, If any man will come after me, let him deny himself, and take up his cross, and follow me. For whosoever

will save his life shall lose it: and whosoever will lose his life for my sake shall find it.

For what is a man profited, if he shall gain the whole world, and lose his own soul? Or what shall a man give in exchange for his soul? (Matthew 16:24–26)

What shall a man give?

Jesus sacrificed His life *for the sake of the Church.*

CHAPTER 3

What Hinders the Church

Much has already been said about the Body of Christ so that some Scriptures might be repeated, but that's all right. We can't get too much of the Word! The Body of Christ is unique; there's no other group, body, or organization that can compare or compete with the Body of Christ. Our God is a God of order. In the beginning, when God made man, He had a plan whereby man wasn't formed until the sixth day. By that sixth day, God had already put everything man needed in the garden.

You may already know the story about Adam and Eve, how they gave in to curiosity and sinned in the Garden of Eden. Nothing has changed about the carnal man since that day; sin is still the cause of his downfall. Sin is the one thing that separates man from God. But thank God for his Son, Jesus Christ, who left his Father's home in glory to come to earth to redeem man, to reconcile us from that separation.

So, the answer to what hinders the church is simple: it is sin. Now, everything done is not intended to be a sin or a hindrance, but the result is sin. Let's look at a few scriptures for the sake of clarity and understanding. Every soul belongs to God, but sin separates man from God. As believers, we must keep our bodies under subjection to God on a daily basis. Jesus said if any man desired to follow him, they had to deny themselves and take up their cross daily. Let's revisit that passage:

> Then said Jesus unto his disciples, If any man will come after me, let him deny himself, and take up his cross, and follow me. For whosoever will save his life shall lose it: and whosoever will lose his life for my sake shall find it.
>
> For what is a man profited, if he shall gain the whole world, and lose his own soul? or what shall a man give in exchange for his soul? (Matthew 16:24–26)

Sometimes, we feel that we can do whatever pleases our flesh, and it will be satisfactory. Let me shock you: It is not okay. It is not acceptable. It is dangerous. Don't play Russian Roulette or gamble with your soul. There's an old saying that "if you play with fire, you will get burned." These are words of wisdom; take heed.

The Bible helps us learn the correct way in multiple passages:

> And as Moses lifted up the serpent in the wilderness, even so must the Son of man be lifted up: That whosoever believeth in him should not perish, but have eternal life. For God so loved the world, that he gave his only begotten Son, that whosoever believeth in him should not perish, but have everlasting life.
>
> For God sent not his Son into the world to condemn the world; but that the world through him might be saved. He that believeth on him is not condemned: but he that believeth not is condemned already, because he hath not believed in the name of the only begotten Son of God.
>
> And this is the condemnation, that light is come into the world, and men loved darkness rather than light, because their deeds were evil. For every one that doeth evil hateth the light, neither cometh to the light, lest his deeds should be reproved. But he that doeth truth cometh to the light, that his deeds may be made manifest, that they are wrought in God. (John 3:14–21)

But when the righteous turneth away from his righteousness, and committeth iniquity, and doeth according to all the abominations that the widked man doeth, shall he live? All his righteousness that he hath done shall not be mentioned: in his trespass that he hath trespassed, and in his sin that he hath sinned, in them shall he die.

Yet ye say, "The way of the Lord is not equal." Hear now, O house of Israel; is not my way equal? Are not your ways unequal? When a righteous turneth away from his righteousness, and committeth iniquity, and dieth in them; for his iniquity that he hath done shall he die.

Again, when the wicked man turneth away from his wickedness that he hath committed, and doeth that which is lawful and right, he shall save his soul alive. Because he considereth, and turneth away from all his transgressions that he hath committed he shall surely live, he shall not die.

Therefore I judge you, O house of Israel, every one according to his ways, saith the Lord GOD. Repent, and turn yourselves from all your transgressions; so iniquity shall not be your ruin. Cast away from you all your transgressions, whereby ye have transgressed; and make you a new heart and a new spirit: for why will ye die, O house of Israel? For I have no pleasure in the death of him that dieth, saith the Lord GOD: wherefore turn yourselves, and live ye. (Ezekiel 18:24–28, 30–32)

I also believe that another hindrance to the church is that many believers are putting themselves in the pulpit and into ministry for the wrong reasons. They want to be recognized and praised for what God is doing, so the focus shifts to what they did, how God used them, and how the audience responded to them. Sometimes, they do not live a saved, sanctified, and holy life, but they can't live that lifestyle until Jesus is living in them. These are wells without water, blind leaders of blind people. They are deceivers of many, including themselves.

Thus saith God the LORD, he that created the heavens, and stretched them out; he that spread forth the earth, and that which cometh out of it; he that giveth breath unto the people upon it, and spirit to them that walk therein: I the Lord have called thee in righteousness, and will hold thine hand, and will keep thee, and give thee for a covenant of the people, for a light of the Gentiles; to open the blind eyes, to bring out the prisoners from the prison, and them that sit in darkness out of the prison house. I am the LORD: that is my name: and my glory will I not give to another, neither my praise to graven images. (Isaiah 42:5–8)

But there were false prophets also among the people, even as there shall be false teachers among you, who privily shall bring in damnable heresies, even denying the Lord that bought them, and bring upon themselves swift destruction.

And many shall follow their pernicious ways; by reason of whom the way of truth shall be evil spoken of. And through covetousness shall they with feigned words make merchandise of you: whose judgment now of a long time lingereth not, and their damnation slumbereth not. (2 Peter 2:1–3; author suggests reading verses 4–22 in your study time.)

Then came to Jesus scribes and Pharisees, which were of Jerusalem, saying, Why do thy disciples transgress the tradition of the elders? for they wash not their hands when they eat bread. But he answered and said unto them, Why do ye also transgress the commandment of God by your tradition? For God commanded, saying,

Honour thy father and mother: and, He that curseth father or mother, let him die the death. But ye say, Whosoever shall say to his father or his mother, It is a gift, by whatsoever thou mightest be profited by me; And honour not his father or his mother, he shall be free. Thus have ye made the commandment of God of none effect by your tradition.

Ye hypocrites, well did Esaias prophesy of you, saying, "This people draweth nigh unto me with their mouth, and honoureth me with their lips; but their heart is far from me. But in vain they do worship me, teaching for doctrines the commandments of men." (Matthew 15:1–9; author suggests reading vs. 10–20 in your study time.)

This know also, that in the last days perilous times shall come. For men shall be lovers of their own selves, covetous, boasters, proud, blasphemers, disobedient to parents, unthankful, unholy, without natural affection, trucebreakers, false accusers, incontinent, fierce, despisers of those that are good, traitors, heady, highminded, lovers of pleasures more than lovers of God; having a form of godliness, but denying the power thereof: from such turn away. (2 Timothy 3:1–5; author suggests reading vs. 6–13 in your study time.)

It's time for us to get out of the way and do what we are called to do. We all must live holy.

> But continue thou in the things which thou hast learned and hast been assured of, knowing of whom thou hast learned them; and that from a child thou hast known the holy scriptures, which are able to make thee wise unto salvation through faith which is in Christ Jesus. All scripture is given by inspiration of God, and is profitable for doctrine, for reproof, for correction, for instruction in righteousness: that the man of God may be perfect, throughly furnished unto all good works. (2 Timothy 3:14–17)

Remember, Jesus came to redeem us, and For the Sake of the Church, He was resurrected! It's fitting and good that we praise Him for saving us and giving us a glorious testimony! Look at the testimony of Romans 10:6–13:

> But the righteousness which is of faith speaketh on this wise, "Say not in thine heart, 'Who shall ascend into heaven?' (that is, to bring Christ down from above:) Or, 'Who shall descend

into the deep?' (that is, to bring up Christ again from the dead.)

But what saith it? The word is nigh thee, even in thy mouth, and in thy heart: that is, the word of faith, which we preach; That if thou shalt confess with thy mouth the Lord Jesus, and shalt believe in thine heart that God hath raised him from the dead, thou shalt be saved.

For with the heart, man believeth unto righteousness, and with the mouth, confession is made unto salvation. For the scripture saith, Whosoever believeth on him shall not be ashamed.

For there is no difference between the Jew and the Greek: for the same Lord over all is rich unto all that call upon him. For whosoever shall call upon the name of the Lord shall be saved.

If you're not saved, this is an excellent time to receive salvation through Jesus Christ. First, repent. That means to "make a turn." Choose to very simply and sincerely turn to Jesus, acknowledge your sins and separation from God, ask the Lord to forgive you and come into your heart, and then thank Him for your redemption through the payment Christ made of Himself to save your soul. Next, you should tell somebody that the Lord Jesus Christ saved you! Confess with your mouth that Jesus Christ is your Lord and Savior. Find a Bible-teaching church to assemble with so you can grow in the Lord and His teachings.

CHAPTER 4

Survival of the Church

There is no doubt in my mind that the church of God will survive throughout eternity. I believe in the Word of God, and therein lies the blessed assurance that Jesus has the power to keep that which has been committed to Him. We have so many promises to help us maintain our focus and remain steadfast and unmovable as we abound in the work of the Lord. *However, these are a few criteria that must continue and be cultivated in order for the church to survive, especially in times such as today.* We must have the *Fivefold Ministry* in operation. Ephesians 4:11–13 says:

> And he gave some, apostles; and some, prophets; and some, evangelists; and some, pastors and teachers; for the perfecting of the saints, for the

work of the ministry, for the edifying of the body of Christ: till we all come in the unity of the faith, and of the knowledge of the Son of God, unto a perfect man, unto the measure of the stature of the fulness of Christ.

While we are all members of the Body of Christ, these are called and anointed servants who walk in their calling. They are God's gifts to the church. I can remember when I didn't fully understand their jobs, but that's why we have to study to show ourselves approved to God. These gifts must remain faithful to their calling and not to the title they may carry. They must know that to whom much is given, much is required. They are the leaders, subject to leadership just as other members are; they yield to the power of the Holy Ghost and continuously desire to please God.

The Apostle, by definition, is a sent one, serving as a mentor to others, going places as the Spirit dictates, and covering his assigned house. Prophets bring unannounced messages from God to the Body of Christ. They speak with the authority of God, sometimes to individuals they meet for the first time. Their spoken word will come to pass.

Pastors serve as angels over God's house. They lead, guide, and are a part of the church family. They must know how to seek God for guidance, understanding, and wisdom in dealing with God's people. The Evangelist brings messages to stir the hearts and minds of hearers. They go from place to place, establishing and assisting in setting up churches. The Teacher is the most overlooked of the Five-fold Gifts; however, it is one of the most needed. Teachers lead and guide in the Word of God. They can explain it to others so that they gain understanding. All of these gifts work for the perfecting of the saints and the edifying of the body of Christ, trying to bring unity in the faith.

We must have servants who are saved, sanctified, and Holy Ghost-filled. Jesus made it clear that we must be born again. That's the first step in preparing a life acceptable to God as His servant. Then, as we learn of Him and grow in His word, the Word works in us to sanctify us. When we have fully accepted Him, understanding our connection with Jesus and His Father, we receive the gift of the Holy Ghost. The challenge for many people is that they are looking for something big to happen. Jesus is gifting them, and they can't believe it happens by faith in the living word of God.

We must have believers who are wholly committed to serving the Lord God Almighty, or, as I sometimes say, The God of the Bible or the God of Israel. Jesus is the God of the living and not the dead. Therefore, our work must always be in the active phase. What we did yesterday or last year might not be what we need for today; since every day is new and God's mercies are new each day, we must stay in the present. John 9:4 says, "I must work the works of him that sent me, while it is day: the night cometh, when no man can work."

We don't have time to reminisce on what could have been or what we should have done. That's why Jesus is so forgiving. He remembers our sins no more after repentance and acceptance of salvation. Every day is a new day with new mercies. It is a day of salvation when the invitation is given to hear His voice. John 3:1–7 says,

> There was a man of the Pharisees, named Nicodemus, a ruler of the Jews: The same came to Jesus by night, and said unto him, Rabbi, we know that thou art a teacher come from God: for no man can do these miracles that thou doest, except God be with him. Jesus answered and said unto him, Verily, verily, I say unto thee, Except a man be born again, he cannot see the kingdom of God. Nicodemus saith unto him, How can a man be born when he is old? Can he enter the second time into his mother's womb, and be born? Jesus answered, Verily, verily, I say unto thee, Except a man be born of water and of the Spirit, he cannot enter into the kingdom of God. That which is born of the flesh is flesh; and that which is born of the Spirit is spirit. Marvel not that I said unto thee, Ye must be born again.

We must have believers who follow Christ's faith and not our flesh. We must live by his faith. Isn't it good to know that every person has been given the measure of faith? "For I say, through the grace given unto me, to every man that is among you, not to think of himself more highly than he ought to think; but to think soberly, according as God hath dealt to every man the measure of faith" (Romans 12:3).

We start with enough faith to move mountains; however, most of us never realize or utilize the power of that faith. You see, no matter what circumstances we encounter, we have been given enough faith to overcome the obstacles. His promises to us are sometimes so simple that we strive to accept them. For example, Jesus says, "If thou canst believe, all things are possible to him that believeth" (Mark 9:23).

We question how we can move the mountain because we look at the mountain with the natural eye. But, when we look at the mountain with a spiritual eye, we realize it is just a stepping stone. It is lower than we thought. It is not as big as we thought, and then we understand that it is nothing to our Savior! As we say, "God's got this!"

God wants us to know the power we have within us. We are living in perilous (tough) times, and we need to know that our relationship with Jesus is on solid ground. It only takes faith the size of a mustard seed to move mountains. That's the size our faith must be!

Furthermore, the Word tells us that nothing shall be impossible to us if, when we pray, we believe God! We have the power of God within us. Jesus abides within us, and the Holy Spirit makes His abode within us! Oh, the joy of righteous, holy living and the things that are within our power.

We do have to pull down some strongholds. We have to fight the good fight of faith. And yes, we must fast and pray.

And when they were come to the multitude, there came to him a certain man, kneeling down to him, and saying, Lord, have mercy on my son: for he is lunatick, and sore vexed: for ofttimes he falleth into the fire, and oft into the water. And I brought him to thy disciples, and they could not cure him.

Then Jesus answered and said, O faithless and perverse generation, how long shall I be with you? How long shall I suffer you? Bring him hither to me. And Jesus rebuked the devil; and he departed out of him: and the child was cured from that very hour. Then came the disciples to Jesus apart, and said, Why could not we cast him out? *And Jesus said unto them, Because of your unbelief: for verily I say unto you, If ye have faith as a grain of mustard seed, ye shall say unto this mountain, Remove hence to yonder place; and it shall remove; and nothing shall be impossible unto you. Howbeit this kind goeth not out but by prayer and fasting.* (Matthew 17:14–21; emphasis added.)

We are more than conquerors; we are the sons and daughters of the Most High God, the King of Kings and Lord of Lords. We are the righteousness of God and the temple of God. We are heirs and joint heirs with Jesus Christ. We are priests;

we are chosen, and yes, we are peculiar! Paul and John are dual witnesses of these truths.

> For as many as are led by the Spirit of God, they are the sons of God. For ye have not received the spirit of bondage again to fear; but ye have received the Spirit of adoption, whereby we cry, Abba, Father. The Spirit itself beareth witness with our spirit, that we are the children of God: and if children, then heirs, heirs of God, and joint-heirs with Christ; if so be that we suffer with him, that we may be also glorified together.

> Nay, in all these things we are more than conquerors through him that loved us. (Romans 8:14–17, 37)

> For he hath made him to be sin for us, who knew no sin; that we might made the righteousness of God in him. (2 Corinthians 5:21)

> John to the seven churches which are in Asia: Grace be unto you, and peace, from him which is, and which was, and which is to come; and from the seven Spirits which are before his throne; and from Jesus Christ, who is the faithful witness, and the first begotten of the

dead, and the prince of the kings of the earth. Unto him that loved us, and washed us from our sins in his own blood and hath made us kings and priests unto God and his Father; to him be glory and dominion for ever and ever. Amen. (Revelation 1:4–6)

Know ye not that ye are the temple of God, and that the Spirit of God dwelleth in you? If any man defile the temple of God, him shall God destroy; for the temple of God is holy, which temple ye are. (1 Corinthians 3:16–17)

What? know ye not that your body is the temple of the Holy Ghost which is in you, which ye have of God, and ye are not your own? For ye are bought with a price: therefore glorify God in your body, and in your spirit, which are God's. (1 Corinthians 6:19–20)

For the church to survive, we must have faithful intercessors. An intercessor is someone who intervenes on behalf of another, primarily through prayer. Intercession, like prayer, involves direct communication with God and requires a continual act of praying for those for whom you intercede. You don't have to be in the person's presence to intercede on their behalf.

I like the way Apostle Michael Artis describes an intercessor. He says, "They carry you in prayer until your need has been met, then they carry you in thanks to God that you have the victory. True intercessors don't drop you; they carry you."

So, intercessors must be serious, concerned, faithful, and dedicated. They will pray when it seems everything is fine, and they understand that intercession is needed daily. Needless to say, they often fast when others are eating and pray when others are sleeping. It takes sacrifice and discipline to be an intercessor because they also have to attend to their salvation as they help work for others.

We must have prayer warriors. Jesus reminds us of a few things about prayer. In Luke 18:1, "He spake a parable unto them to this end, that men ought always to pray, and not to faint." Paul tells us to "Pray without ceasing" (1 Thessalonians 5:17). Also, James provides us with powerful instructions about prayer.

> Is any among you afflicted? Let him pray. Is any merry? Let him sing psalms. Is any sick among you? Let him call for the elders of the church; and let them pray over him, anointing him with oil in the name of the Lord: and the prayer of faith shall save the sick, and the Lord shall raise him up; and if he have committed sins, they shall be forgiven him. Confess your faults one to another, and pray one for another, that ye may be healed. The effectual fervent prayer of a righteous man availeth much. (James 5:13–16)

Those are powerful verses that we often fail to activate. We say, "Pray for me" when we're going through difficulty, but when you think about the Word, do we really do what it says? We should know who the elders of the church are. However, the question has been raised: are they the ones who carry the title, are they the *seasoned* ones, the older ones, or just the Pastors? Based upon the evidence of the Scriptures, the elders should be mature leaders. The elders are those justified by God, anointed and appointed to pray on behalf of others.

The elders then have a job to do. They should pray over the sick one and anoint him with oil in the name of the Lord, and there is only one Lord! His name is Jesus! Notice that it's the prayer of faith that will save the sick one, but it's the Lord who will raise him up and forgive his sins if any have been committed.

Watch and pray! Ask the Lord to show you who the elders are, and He will. They are not necessarily just in your home church. We must be able to reach God through prayer. The apostle James tells us:

> Elias was a man subject to like passions as we are, and he prayed earnestly that it might not rain: and it rained not on the earth by the space of three years and six months.

> And he prayed again, and the heaven gave rain, and the earth brought forth her fruit. Brethren, if any of you do err from the truth, and one

70

convert him; let him know, that he which converteth the sinner from the error of his way shall save a soul from death, and shall hide a multitude of sins. (James 5:17–20)

We must pray that the Lord's will be done. Many times, we pray that our will and desires be done and expect God to answer according to our expectations. However, He will exceed our expectations when we pray according to His will. "He is able to do exceeding abundantly above all that we think or ask, according to the power that worketh in us" (Ephesians 3:20). I'm often reminded of Jesus' promise to us in Matthew 18:18–20:

Verily I say unto you, Whatsoever ye shall bind on earth shall be bound in heaven: and whatsoever ye shall loose on earth shall be loosed in heaven. Again I say unto you, That if two of you shall agree on earth as touching any thing that they shall ask, it shall be done for them of my Father which is in heaven. For where two or three are gathered together in my name, there am I in the midst of them.

There is a tremendous need for intercessors in the Body of Christ, those who can reach God through prayer and who will continue to pray and believe God until the answers are manifest (seen) on this earth. In Isaiah 59, we see the Lord looking for the intercessors. In the whole chapter, we can clearly see the lifestyle of the people and the impact of not having an intercessor. In many ways, the world that Isaiah the prophet was living in was not that different from our world today. Violence and injustice are prevalent in communities, and there is no natural way of escape; however, there is hope and safety in God's only Son!

> For our transgressions are multiplied before thee, and our sins testify against us: for our transgressions are with us; and as for our iniquities, we know them;
>
> In transgressing and lying against the LORD, and departing away from our God, speaking oppression and revolt, conceiving and uttering from the heart words of falsehood.
>
> And judgment is turned away backward, and justice standeth afar off: for truth is fallen in the street, and equity cannot enter.
>
> Yea, truth faileth; and he that departeth from evil maketh himself a prey: and the LORD saw it, and it displeased him that there was no judgment.

And he saw that there was no man, and wondered that there was no intercessor: therefore his arm brought salvation unto him; and his righteousness, it sustained him.

For he put on righteousness as a breastplate, and an helmet of salvation upon his head; and he put on the garments of vengeance for clothing, and was clad with zeal as a cloak.

According to their deeds, accordingly he will repay, fury to his adversaries, recompence to his enemies; to the islands he will repay recompence.

So shall they fear the name of the LORD from the west, and his glory from the rising of the sun. When the enemy shall come in like a flood, the Spirit of the LORD shall lift up a standard against him.

And the Redeemer shall come to Zion, and unto them that turn from transgression in Jacob, saith the LORD.

As for me, this is my covenant with them, saith the LORD; My spirit that is upon thee, and my words which I have put in thy mouth, shall not

depart out of thy mouth, nor out of the mouth
of thy seed, nor out of the mouth of thy seed's
seed, saith the Lord, from henceforth and for
ever. (Isaiah 59:12–21)

We must have saints who remain steadfast and unmoveable, always abounding in the work of the Lord, knowing their
labor in the Lord is not in vain. Life brings on struggles, chang-
es, and seasons that sometimes make us feel as if we can't make
it until the next day. But, thanks be to God, His mercies are
new every morning! That's why we're still here. Many times, we
hear of someone passing away that we thought would outlive
us, but our days are numbered, not by the looks of the body,
but by the grace of God!

So, friends and faith family, we must stay the course, stay
in the boat, and know that trouble will not always last. Weeping may endure for a night, but joy will come in the morning.
Trust God! When I feel outside pressure, I return to The Word
in 1 Corinthians 15:58. It is one of my favorite scripture passages. It is the passage that the Lord gave me for assurance to
proclaim my call into the ministry. It says,

> Therefore, my beloved brethren, be ye stedfast,
> unmoveable, always abounding in the work
> of the Lord, forasmuch as ye know that your
> labour is not in vain in the Lord.

Any time I may have wanted to back up, this scripture stayed with me. You see, we can't determine our calling, nor can we decide exactly how we will or won't answer the call of God. The Holy Spirit must lead us and guide us into all truths. We must not look for the easy assignments but for those that God chooses for us. The road might get bumpy, long, and dark, but if we endure, God will surely bring us out all right! We must be tried in order to ascend to the next level of faith. And we shall indeed ascend!

Oh yes, the Church will survive because it is built on a solid foundation, and that foundation is Jesus Christ, our Lord and Savior!

CHAPTER FIVE

Return of the Bridegroom

> For the Lord himself shall descend from heaven
> with a shout, with the voice of the archangel,
> and with the trump of God: and the dead in
> Christ shall rise first: Then we which are alive
> and remain shall be caught up together with
> them in the clouds, to meet the Lord in the
> air: and so shall we ever be with the Lord. (1
> Thessalonians 4:16–17)

We must be confident that Jesus has a purpose in appearing again and that He will fulfill that purpose. He is returning for His Bride, the glorious Church. Some may say we will be fully redeemed, raptured, caught up, or swept away. Others may refer to this as His Appearing with the saints. You can see all of these in the Scripture above. Whatever terminology we use, the Bible is clear: Jesus is coming again, and His Church will be joined with Him! He is coming to be eternally united with His glorious Bride, the Church, the Body of Christ. The main questions are, *"Who are these people? Who is it that will be joined to Him? And when will that happen?"* Let's examine several passages of Scripture to see what the Bible says.

JESUS, OUR ATONEMENT

Jesus gave His life for the Church, the body of Christ, of which He is the head. We must not forget that all must come to repentance, and all must be born again. There is one Lord, one faith, one baptism. Jesus is the Way, the Truth, and the Life. This earth is not our final resting place; either heaven or hell is waiting for us. Everything Jesus Christ did was *for the sake of the Church!* In Christ, we inherit eternal life, but we also gain the power to live a godly life here on earth. The Bible is our road-map, our GPS, and our instructions.

Indeed, the Word of the Lord is right—Jesus is coming back to get His Church—whosoever will believe and receive Him as Lord and Savior. The question is: *are you ready for His return?* Some will sleep before He comes again. We may not all ascend as a group; we may not ascend as two or three, but in whatever manner it happens that the Lord calls each of us to return to Him, let us be ready.

You see, death can come at any minute. You may have missed the warning signs, but it is still coming. We must examine ourselves and be truthful about where we are with the

Lord. It is time for us to mortify the flesh and put on the whole armor of God. The times are evil, but God is good.

For the unsaved: I beg of you to hear His call to you now, repent of your sins, and ask the Lord Jesus to come into your heart and save your soul! Once you accept Jesus as your Lord and Savior, I promise your life will never be the same again. Once saved, you become a member of the Body of Christ, His glorious Church.

> But what saith it? The word is nigh thee, even in thy mouth, and in thy heart: that is, the word of faith, which we preach; that if thou shalt confess with thy mouth the Lord Jesus, and shalt believe in thine heart that God hath raised him from the dead, thou shalt be saved. For with the heart man believeth unto righteousness; and with the mouth confession is made unto salvation. For the scripture saith, Whosoever believeth on him shall not be ashamed. (Romans 10:8–11)

The Scripture says, "Whosoever believeth on Him." So, first, we must meet the requirements of every Believer (of sonship) set forth in the Word of God. We must believe that Jesus came to earth from heaven in the form of a man:

> In the beginning was the Word, and the Word was with God, and the Word was God. The

same was in the beginning with God. All things were made by him; and without him was not any thing made that was made. In him was life; and the life was the light of men. And the light shineth in darkness; and the darkness comprehended it not.

There was a man sent from God, whose name was John. The same came for a witness, to bear witness of the Light, that all men through him might believe. He was not that Light, but was sent to bear witness of that Light. That was the true Light, which lighteth every man that cometh into the world.

He was in the world, and the world was made by him, and the world knew him not. He came unto his own, and his own received him not. **But as many as received him, to them gave he power to become the sons of God, even to them that believe on his name**: which were born, not of blood, nor of the will of the flesh, nor of the will of man, but of God. And the Word was made flesh, and dwelt among us, (and we beheld his glory, the glory as of the only begotten of the Father,) full of grace and truth. (John 1:1–14; emphasis added)

For God so loved the world, that he gave his only begotten Son, **that whosoever believeth in him should not perish, but have everlasting life**. For God sent not his Son into the world to condemn the world; but that the world through him might be saved.

He that believeth on him is not condemned: but he that believeth not is condemned already, because he hath not believed in the name of the only begotten Son of God. And this is the condemnation, that light is come into the world, and men loved darkness rather than light, because their deeds were evil. (John 3:16–19; emphasis added)

The Bible tells us Jesus was born of Mary, a virgin espoused to Joseph, having come through forty-two generations:

So all the generations from Abraham to David are fourteen generations; and from David until the carrying away into Babylon are fourteen generations; and from the carrying away into Babylon unto Christ are fourteen generations.

Now the birth of Jesus Christ was on this wise: When as his mother Mary was espoused to Joseph, before they came together, she was found with child of the Holy Ghost.

Then Joseph her husband, being a just man, and not willing to make her a publick example, was minded to put her away privily.

But while he thought on these things, behold, the angel of the Lord appeared unto him in a dream, saying, Joseph, thou son of David, fear not to take unto thee Mary thy wife: for that which is conceived in her is of the Holy Ghost.

And she shall bring forth a son, and thou shalt call his name Jesus: for he shall save his people from their sins. Now all this was done, that it might be fulfilled which was spoken of the Lord by the prophet, saying,

Behold, a virgin shall be with child, and shall bring forth a son, And they shall call his name Emmanuel, which being interpreted is, God with us. Then Joseph being raised from sleep did as the angel of the Lord had bidden him, and took unto him his wife: and knew her not till she had brought forth her firstborn son: and he called his name Jesus. (Matthew 1:18–25)

For the sake of the Church and for the benefit of those who maintain some doubt about all of these Scriptures, the Bible helps us to remember Paul's instructions, "Let this mind be in you, which was also in Christ Jesus" (Philippians 2:5).

We must believe that Jesus fulfilled His Father's will in His life, that He did what the Father expected, including being crucified and resurrected. Let's walk through more of the Word, which tells of His divine journey *to redeem us*:

> For unto us a child is born, unto us a son is given: and the government shall be upon his shoulder: and his name shall be called Wonderful, Counsellor, The mighty God, The everlasting Father, The Prince of Peace. Of the increase of his government and peace there shall be no end, upon the throne of David, and upon his kingdom, to order it, and to establish it with judgment and with justice from henceforth even for ever. The zeal of the LORD of hosts will perform this. (Isaiah 9:6–7)

Jesus was about his Father's business at an early age. Scripture says he was twelve years old when he was in the Temple. He was about thirty years old when John baptized him. He lived about thirty-three years, which means he had roughly three years to accomplish all that the Father assigned to him.

> While he yet spake, behold, a bright cloud
> overshadowed them: and behold a voice out
> of the cloud, which said, This is my beloved
> Son, in whom I am well pleased; hear ye him.
> (Matthew 17:5)

Every act of violence against Him was to defeat Him, but He yielded to the Holy Spirit instead of violence. He took the false accusations against Him, the loneliness, knowing one of His own would betray Him and that another would deny Him. He endured the shame and humiliation of being hung on the cross, the beating until blood and water came from His side, and the agony of knowing His mother was in the crowd watching Him endure the sufferings. He even took our sins upon Himself so we could inherit eternal life.

> How God anointed Jesus of Nazareth with the
> Holy Ghost and with power: who went about
> doing good, and healing all that were oppressed
> of the devil; for God was with him. And we are
> witnesses of all things which he did both in the
> land of the Jews, and in Jerusalem; whom they
> slew and hanged on a tree. (Acts 10:38–39)

> He went away again the second time, and
> prayed, saying, O my Father, if this cup may
> not pass away from me, except I drink it, thy
> will be done. (Matthew 26:42)

Who, being in the form of God, thought it not robbery to be equal with God: but made himself of no reputation, and took upon him the form of a servant, and was made in the likeness of men: And being found in fashion as a man, he humbled himself, and became obedient unto death, even the death of the cross. Wherefore God also hath highly exalted him, and given him a name which is above every name: That at the name of Jesus every knee should bow, of things in heaven, and things in earth, and things under the earth; and that every tongue should confess that Jesus Christ is Lord, to the glory of God the Father. (Philippians 2:6–11)

For as Jonas was three days and three nights in the whale's belly; so shall the Son of man be three days and three nights in the heart of the earth. (Matthew 12:40)

Him God raised up the third day, and shewed him openly; not to all the people, but unto witnesses chosen before God, even to us, who did eat and drink with him after he rose from the dead. And he commanded us to preach unto the people, and to testify that it is he which was ordained of God to be the Judge of quick and dead. (Acts 10:40–42)

On the third day! On the third day, *for the sake of the Church,* came **His triumphant resurrection**! Revelation 1:18 says, "I am he that liveth, and was dead; and, behold, I am alive for evermore, Amen; and have the keys of hell and of death."

His walk was not easy, but he walked in union with and in the authority of his Father. His life is the perfect example for mankind to follow. He is the pattern Son and the One we follow after to reach the home Jesus prepared for those who will receive Him as their Lord and Savior!

> Looking unto Jesus the author and finisher of our faith; who *for the joy that was set before him* endured the cross, despising the shame, and is set down at the right hand of the throne of God. For consider him that endured such contradiction of sinners against himself, lest ye be wearied and faint in your minds. (Hebrews 12:2–3; emphasis added)

> There is therefore now no condemnation to them which are in Christ Jesus, who walk not after the flesh, but after the Spirit. For the law of the Spirit of life in Christ Jesus hath made me free from the law of sin and death. For what the law could not do, in that it was weak through the flesh, God sending his own Son in the likeness of sinful flesh, and for sin, condemned sin in the flesh: that the righteousness of the

law might be fulfilled in us, who walk not after the flesh, but after the Spirit. (Romans 8:1–4)

He is the Way, the Truth, and the Life! We can stand on, stand in, and believe every promise that Jesus made. He promised that he was going away to prepare a place for us and that he would return for us (Believer's).

> In my Father's house are many mansions: if it were not so, I would have told you. I go to prepare a place for you. And if I go and prepare a place for you, I will come again, and receive you unto myself; that where I am, there ye may be also. (John 14: 2–3)

JESUS, OUR AVENGER

We often forget that Jesus really suffered for our benefit. Jesus went down into the grave for our atonement and arose as our avenger! However, because of His sufferings, we must realize that *vengeance belongs to Him*, so another purpose of His return is to bring final destruction upon His enemies! Because his saints have also suffered, He will bring vengeance upon our adversary for our glory.

> What if God, willing to shew his wrath, and to make his power known, endured with much longsuffering the vessels of wrath fitted to

destruction: and that he might make known the riches of his glory on the vessels of mercy, which he had afore prepared unto glory, even us, whom he hath called, not of the Jews only, but also of the Gentiles?

As he saith also in Osee, I will call them my people, which were not my people; and her beloved, which was not beloved. And it shall come to pass, that in the place where it was said unto them, Ye are not my people; there shall **they be called the children of the living God**. (Romans 9:22–26; emphasis added)

If it be possible, as much as lieth in you, live peaceably with all men. Dearly beloved, avenge not yourselves, but rather give place unto wrath: for it is written, **Vengeance is mine; I will repay, saith the Lord**. Therefore if thine enemy hunger, feed him; if he thirst, give him drink: for in so doing thou shalt heap coals of fire on his head. **Be not overcome of evil, but overcome evil with good**. (Romans 12:18–21; emphasis added)

Beloved, **think it not strange concerning the fiery trial which is to try you**, as though some strange thing happened unto you: but rejoice, inasmuch as ye are partakers of Christ's sufferings; that, when **his glory shall be revealed**, ye may be glad also with exceeding joy.

If ye be reproached for the name of Christ, happy are ye; for the spirit of glory and of God resteth upon you: on their part he is evil spoken of, but on your part he is glorified. But let none of you suffer as a murderer, or as a thief, or as an evildoer, or as a busybody in other men's matters. Yet if any man suffer as a Christian, let him not be ashamed; but let him glorify God on this behalf.

For the time is come that judgment must begin at the house of God: and if it first begin at us, what shall the end be of them that obey not the gospel of God? And if the righteous scarcely be saved, where shall the ungodly and the sinner appear? Wherefore let them that suffer according to the will of God commit the keeping of their souls to him in well doing, as unto a faithful Creator. (1 Peter 4:12–19; emphasis added)

And I saw an angel come down from heaven, having the key of the bottomless pit and a great chain in his hand. And he laid hold on the dragon, that old serpent, which is the Devil, and Satan, and bound him a thousand years, and cast him into the bottomless pit, and shut him up, and set a seal upon him, that he should deceive the nations no more, till the thousand years should be fulfilled: and after that he must be loosed a little season.

And I saw thrones, and they sat upon them, and judgment was given unto them: and I saw the souls of them that were beheaded for the witness of Jesus, and for the word of God, and which had not worshiped the beast, neither his image, neither had received his mark upon their foreheads, or in their hands; and they lived and reigned with Christ a thousand years. But the rest of the dead lived not again until the thousand years were finished—this is the first resurrection. Blessed and holy is he that hath part in the first resurrection: on such the second death hath no power, but they shall be priests of God and of Christ, and shall reign with him a thousand years. (Revelation 20:1–6)

But thanks be to God, which giveth us the victory through our Lord Jesus Christ. (1 Corinthians 15:57;emphasis added)

He will have the last win, the last triumph, the last glory, and the last of every promise He ever made! He knows everything that happens in our lives—nothing is hidden from Him or too hard for Him to do for us, in us, and through us! But I wonder if we can even imagine what a day in his life was like. How could he face all the many ways he was mistreated as he was walking the path to redeem us? *God's great grace walked Him through.* But because He *finished it*, now the same great grace is available for every Believer.

As the Scripture said previously (Hebrews 12:2), He is the author and *finisher* of our faith. When we're going through our trials and tribulations, let's not forget what Jesus went through, what He suffered for our sake. There's nothing we can endure or face that Jesus is not aware of. But be of good cheer, the Word says, for He has already made the way for us to walk through in victory:

> I know thy works, and tribulation, and poverty, (but thou art rich) and I know the blasphemy of them which say they are Jews, and are not, but are the synagogue of Satan. *Fear none of those things which thou shalt suffer*: behold, the devil shall cast some of you into prison, that ye may be tried; and ye shall have tribulation ten days: be thou faithful unto death, and I will give thee a crown of life. He that hath an ear, let him hear what the Spirit saith unto the churches; He that overcometh shall not be

hurt of the second death. (Revelation 2:9–11; emphasis added)

These things I have spoken unto you, that in me ye might have peace. In the world ye shall have tribulation: but be of good cheer; I have overcome the world. (John 16:33)

JESUS, OUR ADVOCATE

Remember this: just prior to Jesus being crucified, He prayed for us (John 17)! He prayed as our advocate, going to His Father on our behalf. His concern for those sheep He already had gathered to Him didn't stop Him from also praying for those who would come into the sheepfold at a later time—and that included us! That was a foretaste of eternity to come, as, after the resurrection, He ascended to be seated in the throne room of God as our Advocate!

I believe Jesus' prayer for His own may be the most excellent show of agape love that exists. This prayer is for us after He leaves; even in the midst of all that He endured, He wanted to know that we would be remembered:

These words spake Jesus, and lifted up his eyes to heaven, and said, "Father, the hour is come; glorify thy Son, that thy Son also may glorify thee: As thou hast given him power over all flesh, that he should give eternal life to as many as thou hast given him. And this is life eternal, that they might know thee the only true God, and Jesus Christ, whom thou hast sent.

I have glorified thee on the earth: I have finished the work which thou gavest me to do. And now, O Father, glorify thou me with thine own self with the glory which I had with thee before the world was. I have manifested thy name unto the men which thou gavest me out of the world: thine they were, and thou gavest them me; and they have kept thy word.

Now they have known that all things whatsoever thou hast given me are of thee. For I have given unto them the words which thou gavest me; and they have received them, and have known surely that I came out from thee, and they have believed that thou didst send me.

I pray for them: I pray not for the world, but for them which thou hast given me; for they are thine. And all mine are thine, and thine are mine; and I am glorified in them. And now I am no more in the world, but these are in the world, and I come to thee. Holy Father, keep through thine own name those whom thou hast given me, that they may be one, as we are.

While I was with them in the world, I kept them in thy name: those that thou gavest me I have kept, and none of them is lost, but the son of perdition; that the scripture might be fulfilled.

And now come I to thee; and these things I speak in the world, that they might have my joy fulfilled in themselves. I have given them thy word; and the world hath hated them, because they are not of the world, even as I am not of the world. I pray not that thou shouldest take them out of the world, but that thou shouldest keep them from the evil. They are not of the world, even as I am not of the world.

Sanctify them through thy truth: thy word is truth. As thou hast sent me into the world, even so have I also sent them into the world. And for their sakes I sanctify myself, that they also might be sanctified through the truth.

Neither pray I for these alone, but for them also which shall believe on me through their word; That they all may be one; as thou, Father, art in me, and I in thee, that they also may be one in us: that the world may believe that thou hast sent me. And the glory which thou gavest me

I have given them; that they may be one, even as we are one: I in them, and thou in me, that they may be made perfect in one; and that the world may know that thou hast sent me, and hast loved them, as thou hast loved me.

Father, I will that they also, whom thou hast given me, be with me where I am; that they may behold my glory, which thou hast given me: for thou lovedst me before the foundation of the world.

O righteous Father, the world hath not known thee: but I have known thee, and these have known that thou hast sent me. And I have declared unto them thy name, and will declare it: that the love wherewith thou hast loved me may be in them, and I in them. (John 17:1–26)

We must remember that Jesus did not come to condemn the world but that the world through him might be saved. He came to seek and save that which was lost. Ask yourself, "What will it profit you to gain the world and lose your soul? Or, what can you give in exchange for your soul?"

And Jesus answered and said unto them, "Take heed that no man deceive you. For many shall come in my name, saying, 'I am Christ;'

and shall deceive many. And ye shall hear of wars and rumours of wars: see that ye be not troubled: for all these things must come to pass, but the end is not yet. For nation shall rise against nation, and kingdom against kingdom: and there shall be famines, and pestilences, and earthquakes, in divers places. All these are the beginning of sorrows.

Then shall they deliver you up to be afflicted, and shall kill you: and ye shall be hated of all nations for my name's sake. And then shall many be offended, and shall betray one another, and shall hate one another. And many false prophets shall rise, and shall deceive many. And because iniquity shall abound, the love of many shall wax cold.

But he that shall endure unto the end, the same shall be saved. And this gospel of the kingdom shall be preached in all the world for a witness unto all nations; and then shall the end come. (Matthew 24:4–14)

Put on the whole armour of God, that ye may be able to stand against the wiles of the devil. For we wrestle not against flesh and blood, but against principalities, against powers, against the rulers of the darkness of this world, against spiritual wickedness in high places.

Wherefore take unto you the whole armour of God, that ye may be able to withstand in the evil day, and having done all, to stand. Stand therefore, having your loins girt about with truth, and having on the breastplate of righteousness; and your feet shod with the preparation of the gospel of peace; above all, taking the shield of faith, wherewith ye shall be able to quench all the fiery darts of the wicked. And take the helmet of salvation, and the sword of the Spirit, which is the word of God: praying always with all prayer and supplication in the Spirit, and watching thereunto with all perseverance and supplication for all saints. (Ephesians 6:11–18)

Therefore, my beloved brethren, be ye stedfast, unmoveable, always abounding in the work of the Lord, forasmuch as ye know that your labour is not in vain in the Lord. (1 Corinthians 15:58)

And as we have borne the image of the earthy, we shall also bear the image of the heavenly. Now this I say, brethren, that flesh and blood cannot inherit the kingdom of God; neither doth corruption inherit incorruption.

Behold, I shew you a mystery; We shall not all sleep, but we shall all be changed, in a moment, in the twinkling of an eye, at the last trump: for the trumpet shall sound, and the dead shall be raised incorruptible, and we shall be changed.

For this corruptible must put on incorruption, and this mortal must put on immortality. So when this corruptible shall have put on incorruption, and this mortal shall have put on immortality, then shall be brought to pass the saying that is written, Death is swallowed up in victory.

O death, where is thy sting? O grave, where is thy victory? (1 Corinthians 15:49–57)

For as the lightning cometh out of the east and shineth even unto the west, so shall also the coming of the Son of Man be. (Matthew 24:27)

Jesus taught his followers what to expect in their new, born-again Life by teaching about the Kingdom of God. Matthew 22:1–14 records Jesus teaching the crowds using a parable:

And Jesus answered and spake unto them again by parables, and said, "The kingdom of heaven is like unto a certain king, which made a marriage for his son and sent forth his servants to call them that were bidden to the wedding: and they would not come.

Again, he sent forth other servants, saying, 'Tell them which are bidden, "Behold, I have prepared my dinner: my oxen and my fatlings are killed, and all things are ready: come unto the marriage."' But they made light of it and went their ways, one to his farm, another to his merchandise: and the remnant took his servants, and entreated them spitefully, and slew them. But when the king heard thereof, he was wroth: and he sent forth his armies, and destroyed those murderers, and burned up their city.

Then saith he to his servants, "The wedding is ready, but they which were bidden were not worthy. Go ye therefore into the highways, and as many as ye shall find, bid to the marriage." So those servants went out into the highways and gathered together all as many as they found, both bad and good, and the wedding was furnished with guests. And when the king came in to see the guests, he saw there a man which had not on a wedding garment and he saith unto him, "Friend, how camest thou in hither not having a wedding garment?" And he was speechless. Then said the king to the servants, "Bind him hand and foot, and take him away, and cast him into outer darkness; there shall be weeping and gnashing of teeth. For many are called, but few are chosen."

In Matthew 25:1–13, we find Jesus using another parable to illustrate the Kingdom of God:

Then shall the kingdom of heaven be likened unto ten virgins, which took their lamps, and went forth to meet the bridegroom. And five of them were wise, and five were foolish. They that were foolish took their lamps, and took no oil with them: But the wise took oil in their vessels with their lamps.

While the bridegroom tarried, they all slumbered and slept. And at midnight there was a cry made, Behold, the bridegroom cometh; go ye out to meet him. Then all those virgins arose, and trimmed their lamps. And the foolish said unto the wise, "Give us of your oil; for our lamps are gone out." But the wise answered, saying, "Not so; lest there be not enough for us and you: but go ye rather to them that sell, and buy for yourselves."

And while they went to buy, the bridegroom came; and they that were ready went in with him to the marriage: and the door was shut. Afterward came also the other virgins, saying, "Lord, Lord, open to us." But he answered and said, "Verily I say unto you, I know you not."

Watch therefore, for ye know neither the day nor the hour wherein the Son of man cometh.

"Watch therefore, for ye know neither the day nor the hour wherein the Son of man cometh." But He *is* coming, yes, He's coming again! The Bridegroom (Jesus) is coming to receive His Bride (the Church)! Everyone at the wedding must be prepared, including the guests. Perhaps Jesus is giving us time to get ready to meet Him.

Can we envision that, just as most brides prepare for their weddings and work diligently to secure a venue, the gown, food, and the guests, our Bridegroom is securing plans for not only the wedding day but the honeymoon as well?

What Believers know for sure is that *Jesus is our bridegroom*. As we read the Bible, the picture becomes so vivid as to how He has made plans to receive us as His bride. Yes, He has gone to prepare a place where He will receive us. John 14:3 tells us,

"And if I go and prepare a place for you, I will come again, and receive you unto myself; that where I am, there ye may be also." The Lord tells us in 2 Corinthians 11:2,

> For I am jealous over you with godly jealousy:
> for I have espoused you to one husband, that
> I may present you as a chaste virgin to Christ.

This is Christ and the Church. This concept might seem puzzling or unclear if we try to apply natural relationships to our heavenly eternity. Early religious leaders had many of the same types of questions, like these in Mark 12:18–27 (emphasis added):

> Then come unto him the Sadducees, which say there is no resurrection; and they asked him, saying, "Master, Moses wrote unto us, 'If a man's brother die, and leave his wife behind him, and leave no children, that his brother should take his wife, and raise up seed unto his brother.'
>
> Now there were seven brethren: and the first took a wife, and dying left no seed. And the second took her, and died, neither left he any seed: and the third likewise. And the seven had her, and left no seed: last of all the woman died also. In the resurrection therefore, when they

shall rise, whose wife shall she be of them? For the seven had her to wife."

And Jesus answering said unto them, "*Do ye not therefore err, because ye know not the scriptures, neither the power of God?* For when they shall rise from the dead, they neither marry, nor are given in marriage; but are as the angels which are in heaven.

And as touching the dead, that they rise: have ye not read in the book of Moses, how in the bush God spake unto him, saying, 'I am the God of Abraham, and the God of Isaac, and the God of Jacob'? He is not the God of the dead, but the God of the living: ye therefore do greatly err."

He is the God of the living. The passages above teach us that in the eternal ages to come, we will be "as the angels in heaven" as it pertains to relationships, "for when they shall rise from the dead, they neither marry, nor are given in marriage." Why? Because *corporately, we are His Bride*. Earthly marriages don't continue in the eternal realm because it is a *spiritual realm*.

However, we can still learn so very much from how God designed the love between the earthly bride and the bridegroom! Marriage on earth is how God's family multiplies on the earth, but it is also a picture, a type and shadow, that can teach us about Christ and the Church. God created the marriage union to be beautiful, fulfilling, and lasting. Ephesians teaches us that husbands and wives *are to love each other as Christ loved the Church:*

> Wives, submit yourselves unto your own husbands, as unto the Lord. For the husband is the head of the wife, even as Christ is the head of the church: and he is the saviour of the body. Therefore as the church is subject unto Christ, so let the wives be to their own husbands in every thing.

> Husbands, love your wives, even as Christ also loved the church, and gave himself for it; that he might sanctify and cleanse it with the washing of water by the word, that he might present it to himself a glorious church, not having spot, or wrinkle, or any such thing; but that it should be holy and without blemish. So ought men to love their wives as their own bodies. He that loveth his wife loveth himself.

> For no man ever yet hated his own flesh; but nourisheth and cherisheth it, even as the Lord the church: for we are members of his body, of his flesh, and of his bones.

For this cause shall a man leave his father and mother, and shall be joined unto his wife, and they two shall be one flesh. **This is a great mystery: but I speak concerning Christ and the church.** Nevertheless, let every one of you in particular **so love his wife even as himself; and the wife see that she reverence her husband.** (Ephesians 5:22–33; emphasis added)

"**This is a great mystery: but I speak concerning Christ and the church.**" As the Bride, we reverence our Beloved, the Bridegroom, Jesus. We eagerly await His return! He has gone to prepare a place for us, and He will come back to receive us, so where He is, there we will also be.

When will this happen? People often look for signs of His coming, and the truth is that they are all around us! We should be looking for Him to return at any time. Believers can expect that Christ will return because it is written in His Word. Many Scriptures prepare us for His return, including these:

For wheresoever the carcase is, there will the eagles be gathered together. Immediately after the tribulation of those days shall the sun be darkened, and the moon shall not give her light, and the stars shall fall from heaven, and the powers of the heavens shall be shaken:

And then shall appear the sign of the Son of man in heaven: and then shall all the tribes of the earth mourn, and they shall see the Son of man coming in the clouds of heaven with power and great glory. And he shall send his angels with a great sound of a trumpet, and they shall gather together his elect from the four winds, from one end of heaven to the other.

Now learn a parable of the fig tree: When his branch is yet tender, and putteth forth leaves, ye know that summer is nigh: So likewise ye, when ye shall see all these things, know that it is near, even at the doors. Verily I say unto you, This generation shall not pass till all these things be fulfilled. Heaven and earth shall pass away, but my words shall not pass away. But of that day and hour knoweth no man, no, not the angels of heaven, but my Father only.

But as the days of Noe were, so shall also the coming of the Son of man be. For as in the days that were before the flood they were eating and drinking, marrying and giving in marriage, until the day that Noe entered into the ark, and knew not until the flood came, and took them all away; so shall also the coming of the Son of man be.

Then shall two be in the field; the one shall be taken, and the other left. Two women shall be grinding at the mill; the one shall be taken, and the other left. Watch therefore: for ye know not what hour your Lord doth come. But know this, that if the goodman of the house had known in what watch the thief would come, he would have watched, and would not have suffered his house to be broken up. Therefore be ye also ready: for in such an hour as ye think not the Son of man cometh.

Who then is a faithful and wise servant, whom his lord hath made ruler over his household, to give them meat in due season? Blessed is that servant, whom his lord when he cometh shall find so doing. Verily I say unto you, That he shall make him ruler over all his goods.

But and if that evil servant shall say in his heart, My lord delayeth his coming; and shall begin to smite his fellowservants, and to eat and drink with the drunken; the lord of that servant shall come in a day when he looketh not for him, and in an hour that he is not aware of, and shall cut him asunder, and appoint him his portion with the hypocrites: there shall be weeping and gnashing of teeth. (Matthew 24:28–51)

For the Son of man shall come in the glory of his Father with his angels; and then he shall reward every man according to his works. (Matthew 16:27)

For the Lord himself shall descend from heaven with a shout, with the voice of the archangel, and with the trump of God: and the dead in Christ shall rise first:

Then we which are alive and remain shall be caught up together with them in the clouds, to meet the Lord in the air: and so shall we ever be with the Lord. (1 Thessalonians 4:16–17)

And then shall appear the sign of the Son of man in heaven: and then shall all the tribes of the earth mourn, and they shall see the Son of man coming in the clouds of heaven with power and great glory. And he shall send his angels with a great sound of a trumpet, and they shall gather together his elect from the four winds, from one end of heaven to the other. (Matthew 24:30–31)

In John's writing of the Revelation of Jesus Christ (Revelation 22:12–17; emphasis added), Jesus gave the invitation and had it recorded:

And, behold, I come quickly; and my reward is with me, to give every man according as his work shall be. I am Alpha and Omega, the beginning and the end, the first and the last.

Blessed are they that do his commandments, that they may have right to the tree of life, and may enter in through the gates into the city, for without are dogs, and sorcerers, and whoremongers, and murderers, and idolaters, and whosoever loveth and maketh a lie.

I, Jesus, have sent mine angel to testify unto you these things in the churches. I am the root and the offspring of David and the bright and morning star.

And the Spirit and the bride say, "Come."
And let him that heareth say, "Come." And let him that is athirst come. *And whosoever will, let him take the water of life freely.*

Yes, He went from Atonement to Avenger to Advocate on our behalf, and He's coming back to take us to The Father, where we'll live forever!

Thank you, Jesus, thank you, Lord, thank you for being our victorious Redeemer! You gave your life for us. You died on the cross as **our atonement**; in complete propitiation, you were buried in death but arose as **our avenger**, and, by the power of God, You ascended to ever-live as **our advocate**!

Our work now is to be His Body, the glorious Church—with all perseverance. The equipping was in His command: be ye steadfast, abounding in the work of The Lord! Beloveds, by His grace and our obedience, we shall hear Him say (as His Father said unto Him),

> Well done, good and faithful servant; thou hast been faithful over a few things; I will make thee ruler over many things: enter thou into the joy of thy Lord.

For the sake of the Church, **we can finish strong!**

Notes

Endnotes

1   Merriam-Webster.com Dictionary, s.v. "church," accessed April 22, 2024, https://www.merriam-webster.com/dictionary/church.

2   "G1577 - ekklēsia - Strong's Greek Lexicon (KJV)." Blue Letter Bible. Accessed 22 Apr, 2024. https://www.blueletterbible.org/lexicon/g1577/kjv/tr/ss1/0-1

3   "G1247 - diakoneō - Strong's Greek Lexicon (KJV)." Blue Letter Bible. Accessed 22 Apr, 2024. https://www.blueletterbible.org/lexicon/g1247/kjv/tr/0-1/

4   "G1247 - diakoneō - Strong's Greek Lexicon (KJV)." Blue Letter Bible. Accessed 22 Apr, 2024. https://www.blueletterbible.org/lexicon/g1247/kjv/tr/0-1/

5   Merriam-Webster.com Dictionary, s.v. "organism," accessed April 24, 2024, https://www.merriam-webster.com/dictionary/organism.

About the Author

Dr. Mary Ann Shealy Langston is a lifelong resident of Goldsboro, North Carolina. She has been married to her childhood sweetheart, James (Jimmy) Langston, Jr., for fifty-seven years. They are the proud parents of three children, five grandchildren, and three great-grandchildren.

Dr. Langston is an Associate Minister and Secretary at The House of Prayer, Dudley, North Carolina. She is also a Registered Nurse, working as a full-time caregiver. Dr. Langston received her Associate Degree in Nursing from Wayne Community College, her Bachelor of Science in Nursing from East Carolina University, and her Bachelor of Arts, Master of Theology, and Doctor of Theology degrees from Bible Faith Global University. She is a licensed and ordained Minister in the International Association of Ministers and is certified to teach theological Bible courses internationally.

She is also a member of the National Nurses Association and the North Carolina Nurses Association. Dr. Langston has received many awards, including the Nurse of the Year and the Spirit of Excellence Award. Dr. Langston was the Valedictorian of her class.

Dr. Langston is a firm believer that, as expressed in some of her signature messages, waiting on Jesus is *Worth the Wait*, that *It Matters How You Finish Your Course*, that *There Is Power in the Crumbs (That Come from Jesus)*, and that her God—The God of the Bible—is also *God in the Valley!*

Dr. Mary Langston believes that we must prepare to meet our Maker because He is without any doubt going to return for us! Remember, everything He did was for the fulfillment of His Father's will, the redemption of mankind, and ***for the sake of the Church!***